LESSONS FROM THE STREET

VOLUME II

Officer Survival & Training

JOHN M. WILLS

TotalRecallPress.com
www.totalrecallpress.com

TotalRecall Publications, Inc..
1103 Middlecreek
Friendswood, Texas 77546
281-992-3131   281-482-5390 Fax
www.totalrecallpress.com

All rights reserved. Except as permitted under the United States Copyright Act of 1976, No part of this publication may be reproduced, stored in a retrieval system, or transmitted in any form or by any means electronic or mechanical or by photocopying, recording, or otherwise without prior permission of the publisher. Exclusive worldwide content publication / distribution by TotalRecall Publications, Inc..

Copyright © 2012 by: John M. Wills
All rights reserved

ISBN   978-1-59095-659-5
UPC # 6-43977-46591-7

Printed in the United States of America with simultaneously printings in Australia, Canada, and United Kingdom.
FIRST EDITION
1   2   3   4   5   6   7   8   9   10

Any similarity or resemblance to any real people, real situations or actual events is purely coincidental and not intended to portray any person, place, or event in a false, disparaging or negative light.

The scanning, uploading and distribution of this book via the Internet or via any other means without the permission of the publisher is illegal and punishable by law. Please purchase only authorized electronic editions, and do not participate in or encourage electronic piracy of copyrighted materials. Your support of the author's rights is appreciated.

To my Father, Thomas, who left us much love.

About The Author

John spent two years in the U.S. Army before serving twelve years with the Chicago Police Department. He was awarded the Blue Star and the Award of Valor, as well as several commendations and numerous Honorable Mentions. John left the department to become an FBI Special Agent, working organized crime, violent crime, and drugs. Owing to his fitness background, he was chosen to work undercover in the FBI's first ever steroid sting. He also worked undercover in other violent criminal investigations in the Detroit FBI office. During his tenure as an agent, he served in Chicago, IL, Alexandria, VA., Detroit, MI and Houston, TX. Before retiring from the FBI, he spent seven years teaching at the FBI Academy at Quantico, Virginia. He has taught Street Survival domestically and internationally, as well as supervised new agent training at the Academy.

As a freelance writer, he has written more than one hundred articles on officer survival, training, and ethics for *Officer.com*, *LawOfficer.com*, and several print magazines. He is an award winning author of short stories whose work appears in several anthologies. John is also a novelist, having created The Chicago Warriors™ Thriller Series, featuring Chicago Police detectives

Pete Shannon and Marilyn Benson. His books are available online at Amazon, Barnes & Noble, Target, and TotalRecall Publications. His next novel, **_Women Warriors_**, is due to be released April 24, 2012. John also writes book reviews for the New York Journal of Books.

John is an NCAA Speaker, presenting lectures to student-athletes on the dangers of steroids and other drugs. Much of his published work appears on his website: http://www.johnmwills.com and his contributor page at Officer.com. You can reach John at jmwills@hotmail.com.

About Lessons From The Street

I was blessed to have had the opportunity to serve as a law enforcement officer for more than thirty-three years. During that time I experienced emotions that ran the gamut from sheer panic and terror, to unbelievable moments of bliss while observing my fellow man at his very best. I saw life begin, and watched as it ended. I witnessed compelling acts of valor, as well as despicable instances of cowardice and inhumanity.

My service took me all over the world and taught me that regardless of the country cops all had one thing in common—they were Warriors. Police officers held the "Thin Blue Line," that invisible, thread-like, intangible barrier that separates the bad from the good, the wolves from the sheep. The police, no matter what government they serve, allow us to sleep peacefully in our beds at night. And, while often times we criticize and disparage them, they are the first ones we call when we are in trouble.

Cops are sometimes arrogant, might appear condescending or perhaps brutish. Some might even refer to them as knuckle draggers. However, I know from a lifetime of interacting with them that there is no finer group of men and women than the police. The fact that any one of them is prepared to give their life to save yours is something which is incomprehensible to most people. Why would they do that, why work a job that might cost them their life?

The simple answer is because they consider police work to be their vocation—their calling. It's a vow they swear to, an oath that states they will always uphold the law and work tirelessly to ensure citizens they serve are safe, and that their homes and goods are protected. This vow is sacrosanct to cops. The abject proof of their unwavering loyalty to the oath is evidenced in stone on the walls of the National Law Enforcement Memorial in Washington, D.C. The thousands of names inscribed there represent those who so believed in the words they recited when they pinned on the badge, that they paid the ultimate price—they gave their lives.

The following pages are articles I've written and had published in various media. This book is an anthology of tactics, techniques, practices, and just plain good advice for cops on the street. There is no guarantee that sound judgment and good tactics will guarantee that a cop won't get injured or killed, but proper training will maximize the chances that a cop will return home each day to his or her loved ones. Because after all is said and done, coming home is what matters most.

Foreword

When I tell people today that I believe law enforcement professionals should be "called" to their work much like priests and monks or even like the futuristic Jedi Knights – I get looks that tell me just how crazy people think I am. Is it wrong of me to believe that today's police officers and deputies should view their work as a lifestyle? Is it wrong to think of them as peace-keeping and mediating forces dedicated to a moral and just calling? I don't think so; and I'm happy to read the works of John Wills, because he obviously holds a similar outlook.

A great many journalists, media pundits and various "chuckle-heads" will try to convince you that being a law enforcement professional is all about service. They'll try to teach you that virtually everything – from your safety to your values and beliefs – can be compromised in an effort to avoid violence and to maintain a pristine public image. To them I say, "Nay."

Law enforcement professionals – today just as much as centuries ago when the roots of our profession were developed – are warriors first and foremost. More than that, we're a type of warrior-minister if you will, dedicated to keeping the peace with a preference for peaceful enforcement. I don't know a single successful officer who would RATHER fight than talk. In fact, I know a great many officers today who have honed their communication skills specifically so that they can talk people into what's necessary to maintain the peace, just so they don't have to fight. Still, no matter how much they may personally detest violence, it's an unfortunate reality of law enforcement today. Those who prey on the weak of our society won't listen to "please" and "would you be so kind." Of course they won't; they're not kind. If they were, they wouldn't be criminals. So when our police officers and deputies are called to deal with their ilk, it's the warrior peace-maker who has to answer the call.

What all of today's professional warriors know – and John so eloquently articulates in his articles, essays and papers – is that we are all warriors first and foremost. We commit ourselves, our ideals, our morals, our beliefs, our values and our ethics to the service of society as a whole, usually one small community at a time. Together we form what is often called "the thin blue line" but is more realistically pictured as a blue corona surrounding our society; the halo of peace we bring and are tasked with enforcing. As I envision it – in my own creative mind – I think it brings a whole new meaning to the idea of "using the force". We do... together, all law enforcement professionals draw on the energy and support of each other, uniting in our common cause, to protect society's peace and to both serve and defend those who are incapable of protecting or defending themselves from the predators who stalk among us.

It is important that you keep that outlook in mind as you read through this book; an anthology of some of John's work. Remember that what he writes is written from the perspective of a compassionate warrior; a warrior to be certain but one capable of empathy and driven by care and concern for his fellow man. These works are written by a man who has "been there and done that" in places many of us haven't had the privilege to work; the other side of that "privilege" is that we haven't had to conquer the challenges John has. He writes from experience tempered by wisdom and makes an excellent mentor to any and all who would enter the profession.

To those potential brother peace-keeping warriors I say this: read this book. Study the words and appreciate the meaning / intent. If you find yourself in disagreement, reach out to those who are more experienced in these matters to seek clarification or hold discussion. DO NOT assume that what John says is wrong and take that belief with you onto the street where we fight our battle to keep peace. These are lessons he has learned the hard way; the cost has been his tears, sweat and blood. If you're smart, you won't have to pay an equal price for the value of this knowledge.

Read on. Stay safe.

Lt. Frank Borelli (ret)
Police Veteran / Trainer
Editor In Chief, Officer.com

Table of Contents

About The Author 6
About Lessons From The Street 8
Foreword 10

JUDGMENTAL TRAINING SIMULATORS   1
   The Good, The Bad, And The Ugly 1

KEEPING IT REAL   5
   No time for police work 5

LASER SIGHTS, TOY OR TOOL?   8
   Star Wars Technology In The Here And Now 8

LITIGAPHOBIA   12
   The Emerging Trend of Criminal Complacency 12

MAKING THE ENTRY   17
   Slow and deliberate, or dynamic? 17

MY CLOCK'S TICKING   23
   Making a move before time runs out 23

OFF DUTY? – THEN ACT LIKE IT!   27

YOUR PERSONAL DEADLY FORCE POLICY   31
   Can you drop the hammer? 31

PIGS? MAYBE . . .   34
   Porkers among us 34

PLAYING TO THE CAMERA   37

PLEASE TASE ME BRO!   41
   Not supplying all officers with Tasers® is ethically wrong ... 41

PROFILING   45
   Pejorative or Pragmatic 45

PUT THAT GUN AWAY   50
   Are you too confrontational? 50

QUANTIFYING STRESS IN TRAINING 54
Can trainers actually induce the stress experienced in a street incident? 54

SAY WHAT YOU MEAN AND MEAN WHAT YOU SAY 59
Words Have Meaning.. 59

SHOCKING KNIFE TRAINING! 63
Bringing Knife Training Up To Speed 63

SHOTS FIRED FOURTH FLOOR 66
Are you working a one-man unit in a two-man car? 66

SPRAY TODAY, GONE TOMORROW. 70
Is pepper spray obsolete? 70

STREET SURVIVAL 74
Show me the money 74

THE UNSPEAKABLE HORROR 78
"The thought of suicide is a great source of comfort; with it a calm passage is to be made across many a bad night." 78

THE CAPITAL OFFENSE 82
Not training the way you fight. 82

THE DIRTY LITTLE SECRET 86

THE GIFT 90

THE POLITICS OF KILLING 94
Getting shot with paper bullets 94

THE REAL YOU 97
It's not who you see in the mirror. 97

TOO MUCH TECHNOLOGY 101
Are we putting ourselves at risk by having too many gadgets?.......... 101

TRAINERS IN NAME ONLY 104
Five Characteristics of Highly Successful Trainers 104

WARRIORS IN HIGH HEELS 108
Don't test their mettle 108

WARRIORS IN HIGH HEELS, PART II 112
How do their deaths affect society? 112
WHY MORE OF US ARE BEING KILLED 116
What you can do to reverse the trend 116
WILL YOU BE READY? 121
Your test comes like a thief in the night. 121
OTHER TITLES BY JOHN M. WILLS 126

JUDGMENTAL TRAINING SIMULATORS

The Good, The Bad, And The Ugly

Thankfully, judgmental use of force simulators are becoming ubiquitous in the law enforcement and military communities. Having been in law enforcement for 33 years, I can remember the days when the best we could do to conduct scenario based training, was to have one or two staff members function as role players. Then several officers would be given a brief as to what the situation involved; the officers then had to pretend that it was real, use red handle revolvers, and make "bang, bang" sounds to simulate gunfire. You know what came next, the argument as to who shot whom and where.

We've come a long way since those days. We finally graduated to force on force training, using lasers, paintball, and simulations. That was a huge leap, but force on force still lacked several things: enough time, enough role players, consistency, quality of scenarios, and venues to conduct the training and debriefing. Additionally, bringing all of those elements together was a huge task itself.

Enter the training simulators. Simulators have changed the complexion of judgmental training. Giving FATS their due, they revolutionized this genre beginning in 1984. They were the first to offer this revolutionary training, and I for one, was extremely excited about this new method of training. For years, FATS dominated the field, and delivered quality training that filled a tremendous void. Was it perfect? No, but being first at anything is never easy. Now, there are a number of companies that are competing for a share of that market: Advanced Interactive Systems (AIS), Laser Shot, IES, to name a few. Each has its pros and cons, but each brings an element to the training table that will make a significant difference between those who utilize simulators, and those who don't. AIS and Shooting Ranges International have even teamed up to give police departments and military the ability to conduct this training in a live-fire environment.

The courts have recognized the value of this type of training, as evidenced in Tennessee v. Garner, 471 US1, 1985. This decision resulted in court issued guidelines for when an officer can use deadly force. Now that we have guidelines, how do we ensure that we teach our officers to understand and follow them? Of course, we first utilize the classroom, but then how do we reinforce that learning? We do it by using the simulator itself.

THE GOOD

After the legal instructors define your department's use of force policy and deliver the classroom training, the next logical step is the practical application of that learning. As every trainer knows, unless we actually allow the students to have hands-on, that lesson is never fully absorbed. It's one thing to listen to a lecture on use of force, but quite another to apply that knowledge when the officer is involved in a situation that involves, speed, stress, confusion, and threats. Simulators allow us to expose our officers to real life situations that are consistently reproducible for each person. Why is consistency good? Consistency allows us to evaluate each officer the same by having them each go through the identical situation. We then identify common themes and/or deficiencies that we address either immediately, or at a later training session.

Furthermore, the simulators allow us as instructors to view how our officers are likely to react in a critical situation. More importantly, simulator training allows each officer to evaluate themselves: emotionally, physically, and honestly. They can ask themselves, do I have the necessary skills and abilities to survive a deadly force situation? Depending on the system utilized, other training can be incorporated, i.e. marksmanship with handguns and shoulder weapons, low-light training, etc.

THE BAD

Just because a department or agency has a simulator, doesn't mean everything will improve. Depending on the system purchased, you may lack certain options or tools that cause you to continue to have the ability to train your force the way you would like to. Perhaps your budget constraints caused you to get a bare bones system that proves to be not much better than a video game. Or, worse yet you get a system that lacks stamina, is often down more than it is operational, or maybe has content that just isn't germane to what your department does on a daily basis. Merely having a simulator is not a panacea, it must be tailored to the needs of your agency or department, and your instructor cadre must be trained to utilize the system to achieve optimal results.

THE UGLY

It's not a common practice, yet I have seen the following happen: instructors who use a system as their own revenge tool. How does this occur? Instructors will set a student up for failure by giving them a no win situation. The purpose of this little exercise is to cause that student to be humiliated. Another misuse of simulators occurs when the system is equipped with a shoot back device. This allows the instructor to target a student, even thought that student might be tactically sound, so that the student is shot by the bad guy on screen. These two types of abuses should be avoided at all costs, as they make an instructor look foolish and vindictive, but more importantly, it causes a student to lose self-confidence in himself. The simulator becomes a useless piece of equipment to both parties.

KEEPING IT REAL

No time for police work

On a recent visit to Atlantic City, NJ, (this time pleasure rather than business) I had an opportunity to speak with one of Atlantic City's finest; actually it was more like he initiated the contact. I was taking some photos of the Public Safety Building and of a marked unit parked in front. I enjoy photography and take dozens of photos wherever I go, some of which I use to accompany articles that I write. The officer became somewhat curious; alright he was a little nervous and tense seeing someone with a camera taking photos. He braced me, wanting to know what I was doing. After assuaging any trepidation that he may have had about who I was and what I was doing, we had a chance to talk about technology in police cars.

After looking inside one of their vehicles, I was quick to point out the conspicuous absence of any 21st Century technology. I pointed this out to my new found friend, asking him why none of the usual accoutrements normally found in cop cars today were missing. He answered in one word, "money." He said that dash cams, laptops, etc., have been a contentious topic between the department and City Council, the latter always spending tax dollars on "pet projects." The officer said that he and his colleagues would love to have those items, but at this point in time they are happy with just getting a couple of new vehicles every other year. That was the genesis for a discussion about the relative merits of having all of that "stuff" in the vehicle in the first place.

For those departments that are progressive enough and have the resources to purchase the latest in police equipment, a contemporary police vehicle might contain some or all of the following accessories: video camera on dash with full VCR player/recorder in trunk (mike is carried on the officer); radar unit; laptop computer terminal; local police radio for calls within the city; emergency police radio for calls between adjacent departments/agencies; lights and siren—some control panels also have a device that will cause an upcoming traffic light to change to green for safer emergency travel; cell phone; duty bag; emergency lights mounted inside, which are in addition to overheads to provide better visibility; rifle rack; and finally "good time radio" to listen to commercial broadcasts.

Now stop and think about what it takes to operate all of this equipment while driving to a radio assignment or just being on patrol, and it begs the question, "How does an officer still work the street while having to pay attention to all the 'Star Wars' stuff?" Moreover, how do we pay attention to our driving skills while trying to operate or read the computer terminal? How do we safely operate the radio, lights and siren? The answer is with one hand, which is not how we were taught to safely operate our emergency vehicle. But more importantly, how does an officer really get to know the street, in terms of being able to "see and hear" what's going on around him? Does he have the good sense to do what we used to do years ago before much of this paraphernalia was around? Do any officers just get out of the vehicle and walk, talk, and **listen** to the neighborhood that they are working?

I know this is not popular anymore, but getting out of the car leads to some of the best police work that you will ever do. Meeting and talking with folks in the area where you work allows you to really get to know them, as well as the problems that are associated with where they live. Interacting with people, winning them over, letting them get to know and speak with a cop, is the fundamental building block for establishing informants. Ask any investigator worth his salt, and he will tell you that the quickest way to solve a crime is through informants. Having a stable of folks that are willing to give you information about who the bad guys are, and where and who they hang with, beats sitting in front of a computer any day trying to solve a crime. Not only that, but it saves a lot of legwork that it would normally take to canvass neighborhoods.

So while my friend bemoaned the fact that his department lacked much of the modern gear that others had, he was quick to point out that he and his colleagues were definitely "street cops." They spent considerable amounts of time out of their vehicles exploring alleys, buildings, etc., looking for thugs and other miscreants. Would he like to have those big ticket items in their patrol cars? Yes, but right now he gets lots of face time with the people that he has sworn to protect. He and his cohorts continue to get the job done each shift, and pride themselves on "keeping it real."

LASER SIGHTS, TOY OR TOOL?

Star Wars Technology In The Here And Now

The New "Visual Rack" Can Have Quite An Impact

Three decades of law enforcement under my belt has caused me to be a Traditionalist married to convention, especially as it relates to firearms training. I preached the basic tenants of marksmanship to trainees, i.e., grip, stance, etcetera, until they were sick of hearing it. I believed that the manufacturer placed the sights on a weapon for a reason; the sights allowed us to deliver an accurate shot. To fire the weapon without using the sights was an exercise in futility, unless one was only several feet from the target. In the recent past, I have seen and read about sighting aids. These laser devices have been in the form of both internal and external devices that ostensibly allow the user to acquire a target more quickly and engage it more accurately. The whole concept seemed sound, but I was skeptical. Was this an effort to circumvent basic marksmanship? My experience told me that there is absolutely no substitute for firearm mechanics. This was clearly the "X generation's" way of taking a shortcut and showing the old timers their methods were antiquated.

At the Shot Show in Las Vegas, Advanced Interactive Systems (AIS) and LaserMax (LM) teamed to put on a competition that caused me to rethink the whole laser sight issue. AIS and LM put together a contest utilizing the AIS PRISim Training Simulator and the LaserMax internal laser sight. A course was devised in which each participant would fire a Glock 17 or Sig Sauer 226 dry fire laser pistol at numbered balls appearing in random order on the screen. This skill building drill is known as the Sequencer. Each participant was first given a stationary target for practice and weapon familiarization. Next, they fired the Sequencer for familiarization only. After the familiarization, the competition began. First, the time was recorded firing the handgun in the Sequencer without using the LM; the participant then fired the course while utilizing the LM.

The competition was divided into two groups: civilians (totaling 192), and law enforcement/military (totaling 26). In order to cause the exercise to be as competitive as possible, awards were given to the top five shooters in each group. To my knowledge, this was the first time any data was quantified concerning the LM's ability to aid an individual's ability to quickly acquire a target, and then engage it accurately. The result of the exercise for the law enforcement / military group was the average time for the shooter to complete the course without utilizing the LM was 6.76 seconds. When the shooter fired the same course utilizing the LM, the average time was 5.75 seconds. This result indicated a 1.00-second advantage in speed when using the LM.

The civilian group's average time firing the drill without the LM was 7.9 seconds. When the same group utilized the LM, the average time dropped to 6.26 seconds. This resulted in a 1.63-

second advantage in speed when using the LM. One other interesting statistic is the approximate 96% accuracy with the LM, compared to the 75% rate without it. Why is this data important? Considering that many gunfights' duration amounts to 1 ½ to 3 seconds, 1.63 seconds equates to an entire gunfight! That is indeed significant.

During the Shot Show, I spoke with Marshall Schmitt, a retired investigator from the Kansas Bureau of Investigation. Marshall serves as both a law enforcement liaison and analyst for LM. Inasmuch as he works for LM, one would expect him to be enthusiastic about the product. However, Marshall articulated the  advantages of the LM, and almost instantly had me on board as a proponent of this pragmatic sighting system. He quickly admitted that the LM does not replace a weapon's iron sights, but rather enhances them. So what are the advantages of having a LM sight inside your weapon? First, studies indicate that anywhere from 60-80% of police shootings take place in low light conditions. This means that officers are not always able to see the sights on their weapon. The LM allows them to acquire their target quickly and accurately. The LM sights become an asset in times when officers transition from very bright environments to much dimmer conditions. Having to wait for night vision to kick in could be deadly. In addition, as we age our vision begins to degenerate. We start to lose the ability to change focus from distant to close objects. The LM ameliorates this situation by allowing the officer to get on target instantly.

Marshall went on to say that the LM becomes invaluable when used while in compromised shooting positions. These would include officers utilizing shields, shooting from behind barricades, shooting with a non-dominant hand, or having been knocked to the ground by an assailant. Accurate shot placement is attained even though we are in an unconventional shooting position. K-9 officers who typically have their hands full with their canine partner can deliver more accurate fire via the LM.

One of the things I really like about the LM system is that it is internal. There is nothing to jar loose or move out of alignment. Since the LM does not alter your pistol's dimensions, there is no need to purchase a new holster. Additionally, since the ambidextrous on/off switch is not on the grip of the weapon, there is no need to change your grip, and no chance of accidentally turning the sights on.

The LM has a pulsing red laser light as its beam. This feature allows the officer to pick up the beam much quicker than a steady on light. However, what I found to be notable is the effect that it has on the bad guys. Staring down the muzzle of a pistol is melancholy enough, but add a highly visible, pulsating red laser to that equation and the pucker factor has increased exponentially. When the subject glances down at his chest and sees that red dot, we have what one police chief referred to as a "visual rack." Just as many of us have racked the 870 shotgun for effect, so also will many of us begin to utilize the LM's visual rack. I am certain it will have quite an impact.

(Photos courtesy LaserMax)

LITIGAPHOBIA

The Emerging Trend of Criminal Complacency

"Go ahead, shoot me!" Over the last ten years, one would be hard pressed to find an officer who has not heard this refrain emanating from a suspect that is taunting him or her, confident the officer will not pull the trigger. Lately there has been some scrutiny in what appears to be a growing trend by officers not to use force, even when they are completely justified in doing so. What has not been looked at, however, is the effect that this failure to use force is having on the bad guys who encounter the police. There appears to be an increasing number of individuals who show little or no reluctance to assault police officers. These criminals believe officers will not respond with force simply because the officers fear a lawsuit will follow if they do.

"Litigaphobia," the irrational and excessive fear of litigation, first recognized as affecting physicians and psychotherapists subsequently causing them to practice defensive medicine, has now found its way to police and correctional officers. This new paradigm has resulted in officers being overly cautious about utilizing force, even when completely justified. Exacerbating this situation is the systemic fear of litigation from the agencies employing the officers, leading the officers to feel they will be hung out to dry in an effort to protect the agencies' own interests.

The reluctance by officers to respond with force when required to, can lead to catastrophic outcomes resulting in death or serious injury to the officer or innocent parties. Non-action can even engender litigation, criminal and/or regulatory charges, all resulting in the quintessential "Catch 22." You're damned if you do, and damned if you don't.

Given that the bad guys have now succeeded in adding yet another issue that causes our reaction time to slow even further, Litigaphobia is the genesis for what can be referred to as Criminal Complacency (CC). CC occurs when the bad guys become emboldened by the knowledge that the police are too afraid of lawsuits to use force justified by the incident.

In a recent *Winnipeg Free Press* article entitled "Officers Enduring More Attacks," reporter Mike McIntyre identifies 240 documented cases of assaults against Winnipeg Police Officers last year. This number does not sound as profound until you remove administrative officers who do not work the street from Winnipeg's total force. You are then left with approximately 600 officers suffering those 240 assaults.

Even justice officials are noticing the increase in assault cases against officers. "This is completely unacceptable and, unfortunately, becoming more and more prevalent," says Judge Richard Chartier. His comments came after having just sentenced a woman for assaulting a police officer who was trying to take her to jail after fearing she may pass out and freeze to death last winter.

There have been several police shootings where the suspects' action left no option for officers but to respond with deadly force, even though it was obvious that the malefactors would not win. Later investigations revealed no signs of mental history or psychosis. Many times these actions are labeled "suicide by cop," even though there was nothing other than the person's actions in that specific incident to indicate that they were suicidal. In these cases, CC may be the unexplained factor in their behavior.

CC can present itself anywhere along the use of force continuum.

Verbal Non-Compliance

If you speak to retired or senior officers with over 20 years' service, they will tell you that it was rare for a suspect to swear, belittle, or argue with police. They had been accustomed to, with few exceptions, people who were compliant. Speak with an officer with less than five years on the job and you will find a dramatic contrast. They will tell you that they routinely encounter suspects who verbally assault officers.

Physical Assaults

Spitting, shoving, grabbing, and even punching officers is becoming commonplace. Armed with the knowledge that the officer is reluctant to physically back up his commands, the criminal element seizes the initiative and strikes first. More often than not, the officer's unwillingness to use the force necessary gives the bad guy the advantage.

This hesitation has spawned this new phenomenon: suspects that are dumbfounded when the officer does use force to defend themselves or control the subject. Arrestees frequently say things like "They're not allowed to touch me!" or "I pushed an officer before and nothing happened." The bottom line is criminals have become complacent enough in their belief to think that the officers will not respond with force. Would these same individuals walk up to an outlaw motorcycle gang member and assault them, thinking that there would be no reprisal?

Deadly Force

Suicide by cop, recognized in scientific journals since 1985, explains most irrational acts that result in the death of some despondent and/or criminal types. However, there are a number of cases that do not seem to fit into either the homicide or suicide by cop model. These cases involve individuals who arm themselves with an edged or impact weapon and create a stand off situation with police. They taunt police with the weapon, sometimes advancing on the officers to the point of having the officers respond with gunfire.

In the resulting investigations, no evidence is found to suggest that the suspect was suicidal, or had expressed a desire to kill a police officer. Instead, the suspect taunts the officers, edging closer and closer until the officers feel their lives are in jeopardy and respond accordingly. Suspects who have survived these situations related that they did not think the officers would shoot, or that they were just trying to scare the officers away.

Ultimately, police must respond appropriately when they feel their life or the life of another is in danger. Officers cannot try to be psychologists and attempt to determine if the suspects' actions are a display of criminal complacency, suicide by cop, or mental instability, as this can put them and others in harm's way. They need only form the reasonable belief that the threat is real and force is necessary to stop it.

If you, or any officer that you know of, has witnessed an example(s) of Criminal Complacency, please send an email to j.quail@shaw.ca. This article is the first step in an attempt to quantify data in support of this new phenomenon.

This article was co-written by Canadian Police Officer Jeff Quail.

MAKING THE ENTRY

Slow and deliberate, or dynamic?

I am a young Chicago cop with a bulletproof mentality, working the streets and loving every second of it. Most of my street smarts have come because of "OJT," on-the-job training. The thirteen-week academy provided me with little in the way of tactics and officer survival. My partner and I pride ourselves on quick response to any radio assignment, especially crimes in progress and people with guns. This afternoon shift finds us on patrol, looking for anything and everything, when the radio crackles with this all call: **"Woman with a gun on the third floor…;"** the address is just several blocks away. We flip on the lights and siren and rocket toward the location.

As we pull up and jump out, I think to myself, *"Great, we're the first ones on the scene!"* The two of us race up three flights of stairs to the apartment; the door is open a crack, I shove it open and rush in. Much to my surprise and chagrin, I am eye to eye with an old woman sitting in a rocking chair; she holds a double barrel shotgun that pointed in my direction. Why neither of us shot each other seems only to be a product of divine intervention. We eventually diffuse the situation with no one being hurt or killed. However, I quickly understand the meaning of the phrase "**fatal funnel**."

That reckless entry that I made occurred in 1972, yet I remember it as vividly as if it had happened only yesterday. Why? The answer is because we have a tendency to remember incidents and experiences in which we have done something poorly, been hurt, or almost been hurt or possibly killed. Think about it...do you remember when you aced a test, or performed a task in training almost perfectly? Probably not, but you do remember when you failed at something, or put yourself or someone else in jeopardy.

That said, let's talk about making the entry. Unless you are part of a SWAT or tactical response team, dynamic entries are probably your worst option, since they put you in an extremely vulnerable position. They should only be used when other alternatives seem unwise. A typical dynamic entry involves surprise, speed, and violence of action. In addition, these entries should include advanced Intel, positive breach, and some type of diversion or diversionary device.

A slow and methodical approach includes the following advantages:

- Allows time to "knock and announce"
- Allows time to consider tactically sound options
- Allows for the subject to "come out"
- Allows time to utilize cover during entry and clearing process
- Level of training is much less than dynamic entries
- Best used when Intel is unavailable

If you are in a position that dictates you must make an entry, before doing so there are several visual clearing techniques that you may utilize. I recognize that many of you do not want to slow down; you are intent on rushing in to make the arrest. But tactically speaking, hurried entries and pursuits of individuals into rooms, houses, hallways, and around corners many times prove to be deadly. Visual clearing techniques allow for real time intelligence of that room or hallway while minimizing risk. So what are these techniques?

MIRRORING

The use of a mirror is a definite tactical advantage that we as cops must remember to include in our bag of tactical tools. Mirroring a corner or room before entering is one of the best ways to minimize exposure to the bad guys, yet still gather useful Intel as to number and location of subjects, as well as the layout of the room. You want to have as few surprises as possible when you enter into a room. This is especially true if the room is dark, and you are coming from a lighted area. You may also use your flashlight while mirroring a dark room. This takes some getting used to; ensure that you practice before you try it on the street. I used to put my kids in a darkened room at home, and then use my mirror and flashlight to try to locate them. It was great training, the kids loved it, and it gave us time together as well.

Using a mirror affords you great cover while you slowly search the area you are about to enter. One word of caution—if you have used mirrors in the past, you realize how intently you tend to focus on that mirror; sometime to the exclusion of all else that is happening around you. It is best to have a colleague be your cover while you mirror, so that you do not have to worry about distractions. Mirrors come in all shapes and sizes, are flat, round, and even convex for that "fish-eye" effect. I have even used a kitchen spatula as a mirror, rather than rush into a room before checking it out. Use your own imagination as to what you choose, but have something to keep with you so that you don't put yourself on "Front Street" unnecessarily.

QUICK PEEK

This technique is simple and, as its name suggests, is quick. When some speed is necessary, yet caution is still mandated, this technique will work well. A quick peek allows you the ability to get an instant's worth of Intel before entering a room. Sometimes more than one look is necessary; in that case, the second peek must be different from the first. If your bad guy is in that room looking at the doorway, he will see your first peek and be counting on you to stick your head around that corner at the same place as your first peek. Ensure that the second peek is higher or lower than the first. Then, after you have made that quick peek, get into to that area quickly, as things can change in an instant. Even a few seconds can make a difference in what you saw during your peek, and what you see when you make your entry.

If you can utilize a colleague as a cover man while you are doing your quick peek, perform it with your weapon holstered and both hands braced on the wall. This will give you the ability to do this technique even more quickly. Bracing yourself gives you speed; you can perform several peeks in mere seconds. Remember to draw that weapon again before making the entry.

SLICING THE PIE

This technique is performed by utilizing the cover of a doorway or corner and simply moving incrementally so that you can get a small "slice" of the room. The only thing visible to any bad guy in that area should be your weapon and shooting eye. If you do spot a danger area or a subject, you can quickly move back right or left to be fully covered. I like slicing the pie since it requires nothing more than my weapon to be out, and I am in a stable shooting platform ready to engage. To make this technique even more effective, bend slightly at the waist to ensure that your lower body has as much cover as possible. In a doorway, partners can perform this technique simultaneously from either side.

LIMITED PENETRATION

I like to use this technique after utilizing one of the above methods. The limited penetration involves bringing your shooting arm into the room while only exposing your shooting eye(s). A limited pen allows you to cover a subject, or "hold" a room before entry is made, or while colleagues clear a hallway or stairway. If you use this technique before any other visual clear, you expose your weapon to any bad guy in the room that may be close enough to grab it.

SHIELDS

The ultimate entry tool, the shield affords maximum protection while on the move. Used in conjunction with safe tactics such as lipping, splitting, and slicing the pie, the shield is a lifesaver. Much more versatile now, they come in a fold up configuration that allows for easy storage, shields are quickly deployed and make room entries more tactically sound.

Making an entry into a room or house is fraught with danger, ergo the term "Fatal Funnel." Pausing in a doorway gives the bad guys the perfect target with which to take us out. Utilizing a slow, methodical entry, combined with visual clearing techniques, will keep you tactically sound and above ground.

Be safe brothers and sisters!

MY CLOCK'S TICKING

Making a move before time runs out

You hear women discussing it all the time—*my biological clock's ticking, I need to get pregnant before I get too old.* While the odds vary from woman to woman, the likelihood of conceiving and delivering a healthy child declines appreciably after 35 and more so after 40. There is a sense of urgency to "get it done" before it's too late, or risk facing a lifelong reality of thinking, "what if." What if I had a child . . . ?

Similarly, many of us face a time clock when it comes to the proposition of going from a local police department to a federal agency such as the FBI, DEA, ATF, or CBP, to name just a few. Since the federal system requires that  anyone expecting to receive a pension work twenty years minimum to be eligible to collect one, it means the maximum age that one must have attained is no older than thirty seven.

That poses a huge dilemma for some of us, because it's not until we've been on the job for a number of years that our thoughts begin to wander in the direction of long range goals and plans. When we're young and brand new on the job, the only thing that we can think of is our next shift on the street. Indeed, if many of you are like me, I hated for my shift to end. I wished that I could stay out on patrol until I got tired enough to call it a day. Even if I was working midnights, made an arrest, and had to go to court that morning with the thug, I still hated when it was over. I never imagined that there was anything better out there, either in the type of work or the pay that I received.

Fast forward ten years into the job, and my thoughts began to center around what I might be doing in the next ten or twenty years. Would still I be pushing a squad car as a beat officer or sergeant, still rotating around the clock, having days off cancelled, working special events on weekends? The job had lost some of its luster, and I found that I wasn't as locked into it as much as I once was. So, like the case of the ladies' biological clocks ticking, the federal clock was ticking for me. I did not want to wonder years down the road…"what if." I began to weigh my options and discovered that the federal arena had plenty of things going for it that looked attractive to me.

As with anything else, one needs to weigh the pros and cons when contemplating a major change such as one involving your career. A balance sheet is not only prudent in the financial arena, but also when exploring the possibility of moving on to a different employer. So let's take a quick look at what one might possibly gain, versus the likelihood of being in worse straits than before.

The Pros

- Being "Nation wide" versus being confined to a beat or sector
- Enhanced resources for investigations, i.e., money, equipment, manpower, and technical support
- Better salary and benefits

- A pension plan that never goes away (hint…it's the same plan that Congress has)
- Moving around the country
- The opportunity to work anywhere around the world
- Top-notch training
- Challenging long-term investigations

The Cons

- Moving around the country
- Becoming just a number, especially in large offices
- More guidelines and federal rules to follow
- Expectations from bosses and prosecutors that are sometimes unrealistic
- Extended travel and TDY assignments
- Layers of bureaucracy that impedes progress
- TDY in foreign countries that end with the letters "STAN"

Generally speaking you will find that there are more items on plus side of the balance sheet. And, as with any job, there will be things and people that you won't be particularly fond of. But given the freedom that a federal agency affords someone, especially one who may be working for a small department and is frustrated at either the pay or lack of advancement, joining the feds looks like a good option.

From my own perspective, the 21 years that I spent with the FBI was an experience that I'd never be able to duplicate. I worked in several field offices around the country, and was TDY in plenty of others. I spent almost three years working undercover, with so much independence that I sometimes felt guilty even accepting my paycheck (I did take it each payday). My training was some of the best available anywhere in the world. I worked on some of the biggest cases in the Bureau, and spent a couple of years teaching street survival internationally.

Could I have done all of the above with the police department I was with? Certainly not. But don't everyone rush right out and throw in your application with every three letter agency in the country. Examine where you are in your career, and just as importantly, in your family life. There's a lot to be said for staying where you're at, not disrupting your family every few years, and not having to learn your way around a new city and establish your "cred" with a new group of people. At most offices where I worked around the country, I relied heavily on the local PD to tell me who the bank robbers and other thugs were. They knew their town inside and out. And, while the pay will eventually exceed what you are making now, you will probably take a pay cut to start.

That old saying, "The grass is always greener on the other side," means caution—take a hard look. If you make the jump to a federal job without doing your due diligence, you may make a huge mistake. So do your research, talk to folks already working in that agency, and most of all have a fall back plan should you decide that you made the wrong decision.

Is your clock ticking? If so you may want to hit the snooze button.

OFF DUTY?—THEN ACT LIKE IT!

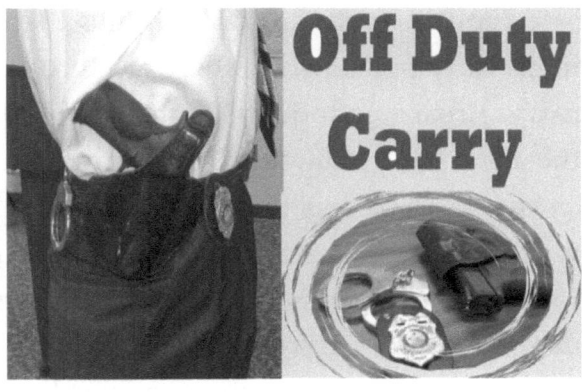

Off duty, on duty, where do you draw the line? Some departments send an ambiguous message to their officers, so that one is never certain about just how much we should interject ourselves into a situation. There are some departments that have policies stating that an officer must be armed and "on duty" 24 hours a day. Other departments leave carrying a firearm off duty up to the discretion of the individual officer. But does the mere fact of carrying a firearm off duty mean that you should still act in the capacity of a police officer? I say no.

Back in February of 2007, Master Officer Kenneth Hammond of the Ogden, Utah PD, found himself embroiled in an incident in a local shopping mall. Hammond had just finished a romantic Valentine's Day dinner with his pregnant wife. Getting involved in a gun battle was probably the last thing on his mind at that point. However, that's exactly what happened to this six year veteran, who thankfully had the ingrained habit of carrying his .45 off duty. Briefly, he rightly got involved and probably saved some lives in the process. Hindsight being 20/20, he later lamented the fact that he had not carried an extra magazine. Furthermore, what of the fact that he did not have any police ID displayed, nor did he have handcuffs? This is not to denigrate Hammond's actions on that day, for he is truly a hero. But "what ifs" are a big part of police work, especially as it relates to having a plan.

Whether or not an officer thinks that he may involve himself in off duty police work, there are three things he should always carry: firearm, handcuffs, and police ID. These three items are the meat and potatoes of police work; one without the other causes us to be less than fully effective. Would you go on duty without one of these? I hope not, for you would quickly see the folly of your actions. So how does not carrying these items off duty differ from carrying them on duty?

How often do we shoot people? For many of us the answer is never. Compare that to how often we put our hands on people, or direct them to submit to our authority, and you have a huge disparity in numbers. That being said, what good is having that gun without a pair of cuffs? Criminals today know that we are not going to shoot them, unless lives are at risk, so without cuffing them how do we stop or restrain them? Just because you announce your office to someone, does not mean they will submit to your authority. Handcuffs become an issue here, on-duty personnel could be a long time in arriving. What do we do in the meantime-hold them at gunpoint? Thugs know better.

And what of the ID issue? It should go without saying that the gun and badge are synergistic. They go together, one has little impact without the other. But an officer cannot have that ID tucked away in a sock or purse. The badge should ideally be in a belt clip worn right next to the gun. Worn in that manner, it causes us to be readily identifiable by either the public or other law enforcement. As was the case with Officer Hammond in his off duty incident, his ID was tucked away in a back pocket; he felt he did not have the time to bring it out. Having that badge right next to your weapon gives instant recognition to other cops whenever we have to act in an official capacity.

And while we're on the topic of carrying off duty, tucking that gun in one's waistband or pocket is asking for trouble. I have been guilty of doing this in the past, but that still does not make it right. If you do decide to get involved, and end up chasing someone or tussling with them, your weapon must be secure. One of two things will probably happen: you will either have that weapon fall out of your pants during the chase and/or struggle, or you will have it taken from you. Neither result is desirable.

The big question now becomes one of "When is it appropriate to get involved?" There is no clear answer except to say that you are compelled to act when lives are on the line. If you decide not to act in a situation where deadly force may be applied, I submit that you are derelict in your duty as a police officer. Anything less than that threshold, you will have to be your own judge as to the level of involvement that you choose. We know that in some instances, it is better to be a great eyewitness. Some of those situations are: anytime family members are with us, whenever we fail to bring the proper accoutrements, and when involving ourselves in a situation that would put us, or another officer at risk.

Knowing when to take police action off-duty is learned behavior. It should be discussed in every basic police academy, as well as refreshed at in-service training each year. Despite addressing this dangerous practice, we still have officers who think it is their responsibility to act on anything and everything that occurs in their presence. I recall one officer that became a nuisance and a danger to his colleagues by virtue of his off duty behavior. The slightest infraction committed in his presence caused him to take police action. Moreover, any officer doing police work was subject to this "off duty super cop" showing up to lend a hand. This can be a dangerous practice, especially on traffic stops when an officer has to take time to ID and control the off duty pain in the neck. When an on duty officer has to take time dealing with this out of control cop, he takes his focus off the task at hand. It can have deadly consequences.

So cherish your off duty time. Spend it with your loved ones, exercise, catch up on chores, go to school, or get involved with a hobby. Whatever you choose to do off duty, ensure that you leave your work at the office. Police work is stressful enough without burdening yourself with getting involved off duty as well. If you are off duty-act like it! Enjoy life.

YOUR PERSONAL DEADLY FORCE POLICY

Can you drop the hammer?

Have you ever been in a situation where you were justified in using deadly force, but did not? After all the excitement died down, and you began to analyze what just happened, did you question yourself as to why you were reluctant to use the force justified by the incident? Do not think that you are unique or strange if you answered in the affirmative. Many of your brothers and sisters in blue have faced the same conundrum.

Law enforcement officers are guided by their departments' deadly force policies. The cornerstone of most policies is that deadly force is used only when it is reasonable and necessary to protect the officer or others from death or imminent serious physical injury. There are other qualifying statements as well, but safeguarding life is the common thread.

Many departments have modified deadly force policies to make them as clear and concise as possible. The officer on the street has to make that important decision as quickly as he can; he cannot waste time plodding through a lengthy litany of conditions. In 1985, the Supreme Court clarified what was formerly a very ambiguous situation for many departments. In Tennessee v. Garner, the court forbade using deadly force against fleeing felons who do not pose a threat of death or serious injury to the officer or others. So now it seems clear, to the extent that a dynamic potential lethal force situation can be, when an officer is authorized to use deadly force.

Now enter the red herring. While not generally discussed, the officer's personal deadly force policy (PDFP) many times overrides his department's deadly force policy. Let's discuss why the PDFP is so powerful. All of us are influenced by many outside factors. Indeed, these things cause us to say what we say, and act the way that we do each day. What are some of these forces that imprint our behavior?

First and foremost is our upbringing. How your parents raised you has a profound impact on the rest of your life. If you had very strict parents, your tolerance for bad behavior is probably low. On the other hand, if your family life was very liberal, and the lines between acceptable and unacceptable behaviors were nebulous, your tolerance is probably much higher. Some households were very strict; the Bible was the moral compass that colored most deportment. Religious training develops a strong sense of morals and ethics that can guide one for a lifetime. A strong father that served as a role model for his children is probably the best example a young man or woman can have. Add into that mix of influencing factors that most police officers have an innate sense of fairness, and you have an individual that believes in giving everyone a fighting chance. Indeed, most officers will tell you that the last thing they ever want to have happen is to be compelled to use deadly force.

Therefore, while we see how family life, morals, ethics, and culture mold an individual's ability to make a decision to use deadly force, there is also another factor to consider—confidence. A police officer can be fully within the law and policy of his department and still not be able to make that decision to use deadly force simply because he lacks confidence in his skills and abilities. He may be a marginal performer at firearms and tactical/role-playing scenario training. In fact, he may be the topic of locker room conversation that questions his ability to perform his duties on the street. Some officers will never be able to employ deadly force, even if their life or the life of their partner is in jeopardy.

I have interviewed trainees with just that mindset. Most enter law enforcement wanting to serve their fellow man. They think that somehow, the deadly force situation will never be an issue for them, but when they finally face reality, they must admit that their PDFP is more powerful than any training they receive at the academy.

Sometimes an officer will spend their entire career without ever having to use their weapon to defend themselves or another. We will never know how many brothers and sisters in blue have served in the ranks that were foursquare against killing another human being. Nevertheless, to the extent that we can know who among us is unwilling to do whatever it takes to do the job, we are obligated to identify them and ensure that when we go through a door together, everyone is on the same sheet of music. PDFPs exist in every officer, but when they adversely affect his or her performance, they become everyone's business. Police work is not always pretty, indeed many times it is downright sad and depressing, but social workers that carry weapons will never work in harmony with those that stand on the front lines every day and night. Warriors need to stand shoulder to shoulder; secure in the knowledge that their brothers and sisters will do the right thing. Make sure that you can drop the hammer.

PIGS? MAYBE . . .

Porkers among us

In Mississippi, The Clarion Ledger reported that the Jackson Police Department is trying to hire more cops, but they're having a difficult time finding applicants who can meet the standards. It's not just that people are having a tough time passing the written exam, indeed, over two-thirds fail the test. But they also can't find people who can meet the physical requirements. According to Deputy Police Chief Gerald Jones, a significant percentage are turned away because they are out of shape. And over a third of the most recent group tested were unable to pass the initial PT test, which consists of pushups, a mile and a half run, obstacle course, and flexibility test.

Sadly, this phenomenon is not unique to Jackson, although Mississippi has the highest obesity rate in the country. It's a nation-wide problem. Captain Michelle Veenstra of the LAPD's Training Division, said twenty percent of their recruits fail the initial fitness test. But rather than discarding them, they enlist them in a special program, directing their workouts and educating them about nutrition and the importance of fitness. A similar approach is taken by the FBI in their initial testing. When they've identified applicants likely to attend new agent training, they are tested in the field to see if they'll be able to pass the first PT test at Quantico's FBI Academy. If they're found lacking in a certain dimension, such as cardio or strength, they are given specific exercises to correct the deficiency. Yet even after the one-on-one attention, trainees continue to report for training, unable to pass with a minimum score.

This boggles my mind. I can't imagine applying for a job that you know requires you be in probably the best shape of your life. How can people report for training, overweight and out of shape? It defines one's character and work-ethic, and it's a reflection of society, in that we frown on strict requirements and want everyone to be a winner—medals and trophies to all. Heaven forbid we should turn someone away simply because they can't run a mile and a half. They're entitled to that job.

In a study conducted by researchers at Harvard and Boston Universities, and the Cambridge Health Alliance, it was found that 77% of fire and EMT trainees in Massachusetts were overweight or obese. The lead author, Tony Tsismenakis, said the percentage is probably even higher, since the research did not include applicants who were disqualified for fitness.

Professor Stefanos Kales, Harvard School of Public Health, participated in the same study. He noted that, "No national studies on recruits exists, but in localized studies researchers consistently find that among police and firefighters, generally three-quarters are overweight, and that includes one-third that are obese." He paints a bleak picture about the future, saying, ". . . over the years, some departments have lowered physical strength standards to avoid discrimination lawsuits. In combination with a less-fit pool, that will end up allowing more obese recruits to successfully join these services."

According to APP.com, in Lawton, Oklahoma, Chief Ronald Smith said about 15% of applicants this spring failed an initial agility test, including pushups and a quarter-mile run. "Used to be nearly 100% passed the agility test." And in Jefferson City, Missouri, Captain Doug Shoemaker said, "A noticeable number of people failed the physical exam in the two most recent tests."

How do we fix the problem? Some think it's an education-based solution. According to a <u>report in USA Today,</u> Texas Christian University kinesiology professor Deborah Rhea, blames it on cuts in school PE programs. She said PE classes are a must as part of the curriculum. "You've got to educate them (about) why they need to be active." I agree with that premise—too much technology and not enough exercise and intramural activities. The PC-types have outlawed dodge ball, tag, touch-football, and just about anything else that requires running and agility. No wonder we have young adults who can't lift their own body weight. Not only do schools enforce zero-tolerance for guns and drugs, it seems the same applies for any activity in which the student must exert themselves. Playgrounds are an anachronism.

I don't think the solution can be found in lowering the bar any more than it already is—it's just about resting on the ground. Having been a part of a system that tested and trained new agents, I think it's imperative that standards be maintained and met, without regard to who one may know, gender, race, or any other red herring one may want to throw into the mix. Either you pass or you fail. Simple. The requirements are plainly spelled out for all to read and comprehend before an application is completed. PT standards are not kept secret, nor are they fluid, that's why they call them standards.

I suggest we all face reality: our nation is becoming soft and weak. The reason: no backbone. The solution: don't abdicate your responsibility, either as an administrator, a cop, or an applicant for the job. Being fit may one day save your life—or mine.

PLAYING TO THE CAMERA

Lately I've seen some strange photos and videos posted on the internet. Many of the pictures and movies that appear on certain websites are obscene in my estimation, yet there they are for everyone to see. People are caught in humiliating and embarrassing situations; some of them appear to be willing participants while others seem to be unaware that a lens is pointed in their direction. It's this latter group that I refer to in this article.

The ubiquitous camera; one cannot seem to escape its reach. We are being constantly monitored from the time we leave our homes, until we finally return. And even then some of us have cameras on both the outside and inside of our property. It seems that there is not one place where we can escape and breathe a sigh of relief. Schools, churches, supermarkets and malls, they are all equipped with cameras. The big cities have them. New York and Chicago put cameras up in busy downtown areas and in high crime neighborhoods, hoping to spot those that break the law. And don't forget the speed and red light cameras that are in vogue. Money makers for sure, but are all of these cameras good for society? And does the presence of so many recording devices cause all of us to change our normal behavior?

I know that I date myself when I tell you that when I first became a cop the last thing on our mind was whether someone was taking our picture. Cameras were not cheap; moreover the ability to develop and print the film was an expensive laborious process. Generally speaking it took several days to get a look at the finished product. Videos? Forget about it. No one took videos because the cameras were burdensome to carry and operate. Lighting was a problem; one needed to have an annoyingly bright light mounted on top of the camera to illuminate the subject. In short it was best left to the professionals.

Fast forward to 2008...who doesn't have a camera? Little children are walking around with cell phones, all of which are capable of taking both photos and videos. Storage media in the form of digital images not only allows for instant results, but now anyone can edit a photo to change it from its original form to something entirely different (Can you say Photoshop?) Photos used to be best evidence in court, now their credibility is easily challenged.

So what does this mean to you as a police officer? How has your behavior changed, or has it remained the same? One aspect of this picture-crazed society that we live in is that you must now include the possibility of your actions being recorded whenever you respond to an incident. Are you reacting to a situation as your training and experience dictates, or are you acting differently because you see someone with a camera, or suspect that someone may be taping you? This has a direct effect on your reactionary time. It's not unlike being in a deadly force situation and waiting to act because you are worried about how your actions will be portrayed on the evening news. It all serves to limit your ability to act and react quickly.

Now the moral question about your actions that begs to be asked: Would your behavior be the same whether or not cameras were involved? Were you previously acting in a manner that was improper or unethical, but now the possibility that you may be filmed has that caused you to act more appropriately? Are you now simply playing to the camera?

Trainers see this phenomenon all the time. Put two or three people in a scenario, perhaps in a simulator, and we often see atypical behavior. Throw in a supervisor to observe them as they go through a scenario, and the atypical behavior is even more pronounced. What actually occurs is that the officers behave in a manner in which they think either the evaluator or the supervisor expects them to act. They aren't their normal selves, they are acting out. The danger of course is that the principle that says, "The way you train is the way you fight," is violated. Ergo, when they are confronted with the same situation on the street their reaction time is adversely impacted causing them to be further behind the power curve. That can get you hurt or killed.

So what's the answer? How do we navigate through this camera laden society without it having too much of an impact on us? If you look at it from the perspective of cameras as impartial observers, especially dash cams, they can actually work in our favor. More than one officer has seen a beef thrown out due to dash cam evidence refuting whatever the complainant had to say.

I submit that the way to avoid most problems of this nature is to act responsibly and morally—just be you. There will be times when you have to thump somebody—we're cops, it's the nature of the job. It's when we give them that extra smack that they didn't need. It's when we give them that boot in the butt after the cuffs are on that we expose ourselves to litigation and prosecution. Remember we are not the judge and jury; rather we are the keepers of the peace. We are the ones that sort out the confusion and bring those most responsible to the arbiters of the law. They will decide on punishment or mercy. If you do the right thing, the rest of it will take care of itself.

PLEASE TASE ME BRO!

Not supplying all officers with Tasers® is ethically wrong

A recent article in USA Today written by Kevin Johnson was posted on Officer.com in April. The article, <u>Better Defense Tactics Helping to Curb Law Enforcement Deaths,</u> was premised on the fact that since there has been more of an emphasis on defensive tactics training, police deaths have been cut in half this year when compared to the spike in line of duty (LOD) deaths in 2007. Thankfully, LOD deaths have decreased so far this year, but my sense is that better DT training is only a small part of the answer.

Defensive tactics has been around for years in one form or another. One of the problems that police departments have had is the reactive stance that we assume in most of our training. Until some tragedy occurs that causes us to reassess our training, we continue to utilize the same tactics year in and year out. The big reason for that, more often than not, is money. Whenever a trainer learns of a new way to do something more effectively, safer, or quicker, the first question the admin folks ask is, "How much will this cost to train our department?"

One big exception to that general rule is ground fighting. In the last several years, most departments have included this skill set in their DT curriculum. For the longest time we used to put boxing gloves on trainees and let them knock the snot out of each other. For all the time and money spent on that pursuit, the rewards never materialized. The only thing of value realized from that exercise was that some trainees that had never been hit before finally had an idea of what to expect on the street. Ground fighting is much more of a practical skill to teach. Ask any DT Instructor or working street cop, and they will tell you that after a punch or two is thrown, everything is going down to the ground. Thanks Royce Gracie.

Technology has enabled us to grow the number of options that we can reach for when confronted by the bad guys. Before chemical agents debuted, we either used our night sticks (now called batons) or went toe to toe with non-compliant folks. Fisticuffs are definitely the "manly" way of compelling a person to cooperate. Unfortunately many of us couldn't punch our way out of a paper bag. We either wound up getting our clocks cleaned, had a heart attack from the shock and exertion involved, or put ourselves in danger of having our weapon taken away.

Mace and OC allowed us to take a somewhat safer approach by standing back and spraying. Of course the downside was that not everyone was affected by the spray, except for the officer and his partners, so you could never guarantee that it would be effective. Additionally, some officers have an expectation that the spray will incapacitate someone—it doesn't, it give us the opportunity to jump into the gap created to regain control. However, it was still a good idea to have another less lethal option available.

Enter the Taser®; probably the most effective and safest less lethal weapon to emerge on the law enforcement scene in years. In my opinion, the Taser is the reason why LOD deaths have decreased. The Taser's® effectiveness has resulted in fewer hand to hand combat incidents. The more often that we can deal with non-compliant subjects at an arm's length, the safer we remain. Inasmuch as Taser® has now become a household word, especially since the infamous words, "Don't tase me bro" were spoken by the imbecile at the University of Florida in September of 2007, the Taser® has developed a reputation on the street that makes it a formidable weapon. Incidentally, for those that don't know, the student involved in that Taser® incident eventually admitted that his actions were out of line. He apologized and conceded that the officers did nothing wrong. All his charges will be dismissed if he completes an 18 month probation period.

Given the Taser's® effectiveness on non-compliant subjects, and the fact that it has saved many of our officers from having to go hands on with cretins that won't take no for an answer, why is it that some jurisdictions refuse to supply this great tool to the guys and gals on their department? Fewer physical confrontations means fewer job related injuries and thus fewer workman's comp claims. According to Taser's® website, police departments have experienced anywhere from 25-80% reduction in officer injuries. Hey folks, we're not getting paid to get hurt by knuckle draggers. DT training is fine, and must continue to be emphasized, but Tasers are the way to go. They are the technology that helps keep cops on the road, not in the emergency rooms.

New York, New Jersey, Rhode Island, and all the other states that have not approved the use of Tasers® by their officers, in my opinion, are being ethically disingenuous. From either the perspective of the officers' themselves, or the citizenry that will be on the receiving end of this technology, it is morally incorrect not to include this in the use of force continuum. If I am facing someone larger than myself who refuses to obey my commands, more often that not I will choose the Taser® to gain compliance.

I dare say that most officers would opt to do so as well, over hand to hand, OC, or baton. Why are LOD deaths down this year compared to 2007? The Taser®!

Taser stats on officer injuries
http://taser.com/Pages/le_overview.aspx

USA Today 4/21/08
http://officer.com/web/online/Top-News-Stories/Better-Defense-Tactics-Helping-to-Curb-Law-Enforcement-Deaths/1$41099

PROFILING

Pejorative or Pragmatic

The politically correct (PC) crowd has succeeded in emasculating some of our law enforcement tools and tactics under the guise of profiling. The most obvious and blatant example of this is at our nation's airports. The Transportation Security Authority (TSA) has standing orders not to profile Muslim passengers, deliberately not taking them out of line for either questioning or a more thorough search, since that would be "profiling." Instead, the preferred PC tactic is to "randomly" select passengers in general for a more complete screening. That results in the ridiculous, humiliating sight of 80-year-old grandmothers in wheelchairs, infants in diapers, our heroic military personnel in full uniform, and frequent traveler business types, being wanded and their carry-ons inspected. Then, add to that debacle the public observing this completely sordid affair, and you have one big cluster at our nation's airports, just so that no one feels uncomfortable. That really means so that Muslims do not feel singled out or targeted. Someone please tell me if I am wrong, but in the past ten years hasn't 99.9% of all terrorist attacks and threats been committed by Muslims? Not to profile them seems to be a dereliction of duty.

In any basic police academy, recruits learn the most efficient and expeditious way to investigate a crime is to look for the most logical suspects. Generally speaking, police categorize, profile, discriminate, whatever term you care to use, criminals into categories or types. These types of criminals exhibit certain behaviors that coincide with their criminal acts. For example, drug dealers like to wear gaudy, huge, obnoxious looking jewelry (aka bling) as part of their official uniform. If an officer on patrol spots one of these individuals, he generally assumes this subject is a drug dealer. These drug entrepreneurs travel in luxury type vehicles—BMWs, Mercedes, and Lexus, as well as SUVs. The officer can count on these guys or one of their associates—usually female—to be holding drugs, money, or guns. That is what is known as profiling, typing, or categorizing. Where I come from it is also known as street smarts, and it allows cops to quickly identify and separate the good guys from the bad guys. Incidentally, the bad guys do the same thing, they profile us. Just as they make it easy for us to spot them, by their dress, hair styles, tattoos, etc., we wear uniforms, have short hair, and much to their dismay, see everything going on around us. They spot us by our vehicles and behavior, catching us rubbernecking as we drive down the street.

Profiling is the most basic of skills that an officer must master if he is to be a success at his profession. It makes our job easier, and it eliminates wasted time and resources looking for someone that played no part in the matter that we are investigating. If a bank robbery was committed by two thin white males in their early 20's, wearing baseball hats and sneakers, why would a cop stop an elderly black person wearing a suit, and question him in regard to the crime? It doesn't make sense does it?

If a neighborhood has been besieged by prostitutes, most of which are attired in clothing that barely covers the parts of their bodies that their mothers warned them to always keep covered, would any smart cop question an old lady walking down the street with a shopping cart about prostitution? If that happened, either that cop is a Mayberry reject or TSA brainwashed. Regardless, he has no business being a cop, since he ignores the most rudimentary tool used by all of law enforcement—profiling. Talking to, and investigating the most likely people that may have, or are about to commit a crime, enables us to arrest and detain those that are the most likely offenders.

Think about how important this whole concept and practice of profiling is to law enforcement. Some of the most heinous crimes committed in our otherwise lawful society, would never have been solved without the skills of a professional profiler. When cops are stymied in their investigation, and have no idea of who may have committed the crime, they turn the case over to profilers. In my own experience, the FBI profilers that worked out of the Behavioral Science Unit (BSU) at Quantico, Virginia, were instrumental in solving dozens of cases. Local authorities turned over case files that were cold, all leads exhausted, in hopes that the profilers might give them an insight into a subject to pursue and therefore help the investigators solve the crime. On some occasions the profiles may have been wrong, but most times the profile developed by the guys and gals in the BSU injected new life into the case.

Why is profiling acceptable in other professions, but not in ours? The auto insurance companies profile drivers all the time. Young drivers under the age of 25, unmarried drivers,

drivers that have had driving convictions and accidents, all these profiled types have higher insurance rates. They are "singled out" as poor risks. The medical profession profiles as well. Certain races and sexes are more prone to different diseases, i.e. heart attacks and strokes—that's profiling. Some people who have family histories of cancer are singled out for further screening—that's profiling. Attorneys profile all the time. Next time you watch TV, count how many commercials you see for law firms trying to help you sue doctors and hospitals over alleged poor medical care—that's profiling folks. The lawyers know that a certain group of people are likely to want their services.

Do we profile when we watch traffic? Of course! When we see a driver weaving in and out of lanes, speeding, or conversely, driving 20 miles under the speed limit—we profile them and place them in the category of likely driving while impaired. We profile certain types of vehicles and drivers, on certain roads and Interstates. We know that certain vehicles are known to carry illegal drugs and cash on certain north/south routes on the East coast. That is profiling, and that practice has led to huge seizures of drugs and cash.

How do you ignore behaviors, people, and instruments of crime, when from your past experience you can prove that they have led to criminal activity? Moreover, if you did ignore these "clues," these positive indicators that a crime has been, or is about to be committed, how long would the people that hired you continue to employ you? I suspect that the answer would be that you would be gone for ignoring fundamentals about police work. Yet that is what is being done today. The PC crowd continues to assail law enforcement for anything that they believe to be profiling. People who accuse anyone of profiling them are considered victims. Anyone who is made to feel uncomfortable due to a profile is awarded huge sums of money (they themselves were profiled by the lawyers). Yet when crimes are committed, or large-scale tragedies occur, the first ones to point the finger at us for not preventing it from happening are the very PC types that outlawed our ability to be proactive in the first place! So the paradox of profiling continues, it is both a pragmatic tool and a pejorative practice. You figure it out; my head is splitting.

PUT THAT GUN AWAY

Are you too confrontational?

The <u>Washington Metropolitan Police Department</u>, a superb organization defending our nation's capital, patrols a unique landscape. The White House, The Capitol, and the dozens of monuments that populate the area, make for an attractive backdrop. During business hours, thousands of government workers swarm the buildings and streets, barely requiring any policing. Yet when the mass exodus of those employees occurs at five o'clock in the afternoon, and they all head home to the suburbs, the District takes on an entirely different complexion.

Last year in a city with a population of just over half a million, there were 143 homicides; in 2008, a total of 186, this, in a city that formerly prohibited gun ownership. Since lifting the ban, there have been 43 fewer homicides. Coincidence? You decide, but I think whenever citizens are denied the right to bear arms, only the bad guys have guns. In Washington when the sun goes down, the thugs come out to play. Those ambassadors of DC who ensured the city ran smoothly for the temporary day-residents, must now steel themselves to do battle with the knuckle-draggers who come out to prey on the law-abiding residents of the District.

No big deal, that's what we do as cops. We train and prepare ourselves for those scenarios and confrontations that will likely present themselves. Crime prevention means not only structured programs to inform and educate, but it also means having aggressive, street-smart cops on the beat, who by their very appearance and demeanor demonstrate to the cretins on the street that "cops run it." Just as the bad guys intimidate and frighten their victims to capitulate, so also do the well-trained, experienced, aggressive cops present that same image to the thugocracy who think the streets belong to them.

Why do I feel the need to write about this obvious fact of police life? Because today <u>it was reported</u> that a DC cop is facing a ten day suspension for drawing his weapon at a snowball fight. On February 4th, the MPD's internal affairs said the officer acted "confrontational" as he approached a large crowd. Well, I guess any one of us might pull our gun if, as the report states, the group had clubs and shields. In fact, a couple of minutes later a marked unit arrived and a uniformed officer wisely approached the group, also with his weapon drawn at his side.

The back-story is that the officer was off-duty (which I've always found to be a conundrum since we're expected to take police action 24/7, meaning we're always on-duty) when a man threw a snowball at him. The cop got out of his car and moved toward a large crowd gathered at the intersection. As he approached, he unholstered his weapon—good police work in my estimation—let 'em know who you are and that you mean business.

Here's where the incident takes the inevitable IAD twist. Officials now want to suspend him, not so much for having his weapon out, but for not reporting the man he thought had thrown the snowball at him. Because popular sentiment no longer favors disciplining a cop for pulling his gun, the department decided to obfuscate the issue by turning into a technical issue . . . a policy violation. I've always said, follow any good street cop during his tour and you're bound to find a policy violation somewhere. Apply that same scrutiny to the bosses—bigger fish—bigger violations. The bottom line: if they want to get you, they can and will.

This backtracking, this convoluted way of getting their pound of flesh, is what's most disconcerting to me. By all accounts, the cop is an experienced, street-smart detective. He knows how to handle thugs and incidents likely to get out of hand. He knows that a show of force will often times de-escalate a situation. His backup unit was on the same page.

As is the case in our technological society, several people had cameras and phones on that day. Some videoed the incident and it appeared on the internet. It clearly shows one man against a hostile group of idiots, a mob that was probably about to quench its thirst for trouble by continuing their inappropriate behavior. The cops would be called, eventually. The incident garnered national attention, and was sensationalized by those who have no clue about what happens in the real world, by characterizing it as a cop threatening innocent people throwing snowballs.

However, here is the bigger question: What if they had confronted an innocent citizen who had neither the means nor vigor to defend himself? What then? I contend that tough cops, when the appropriate situation is at hand, are the best defense. Most thugs are cowards when confronted individually. But when they congregate and form into a gang, that dynamic changes. The only thing that works on those types is force, or at least the threat of it. It's the law of the jungle, and all of the rhetoric about the poor, disadvantaged punks who relish challenging authority is bunk.

I hate seeing this incident mushrooming into what it has now become. With so much publicity, neither side is likely to acquiesce. My fear is that good cops will look at the outcome and be reticent to pull their guns at times when it is imperative they do so. We train our officers to be ready, to be proactive, to stay ahead of the power curve. If we discipline our cops for simply pulling their weapon and having it at the ready when they feel threatened, we send the wrong message. We cause our guys and gals to become timid, while emboldening the cretins on the street.

My recommendation is this: don't change the way you're operating because of one bad call. You owe it to all of us to be the best cops you can be—that means being aggressive and tough when need be. I have no clue as to how this *gun versus snowball* issue will be resolved. However, if we begin to see officers and departments sanctioning "guns out of holsters," we are most certainly heading down the wrong road.

QUANTIFYING STRESS IN TRAINING

Can trainers actually induce the stress experienced in a street incident?

We know the importance of training in police work as it relates to our survival. Anyone who is not familiar with the axiom, "The way you train, is the way you fight," has probably been hiding underneath a rock somewhere in the mountains. Stress influences the way we react to situations on the street. What we as trainers need to understand, and subsequently structure our courses to combat, is to somehow replicate that stress, and train our officers to win, in spite of the deleterious effects that stress has on our performance.

In 1998, Bruce Siddle conducted research involving officers in an identical training scenario with various stressors included. There are not many studies of this kind, since controlling all of the variables and quantifying results is an enormous task. Nevertheless, Siddle embarked on this ground breaking journey, and titled the work, "Combat Human Factors: Triggering the Survival Circuit."

In the study, he discussed a great many things, to include how we shoot. He compared and contrasted Isosceles and One Hand Point shooting, as they relate to close quarter combat. These two types of shooting styles were developed in the 1920's, the purpose of which was to promote quick response type shooting without using the sights. The two systems have been tested and refined since then, and have been proven to be highly effective techniques for survival. Interestingly, after

Siddle's study was conducted of the officers involved in a stress-induced scenario, more than half resorted to an Isosceles/Modified Isosceles stance, i.e., squared up to the threat, even though the vast majority of the participants in the study were trained to shoot in the asymmetrical Weaver stance, which is a bladed technique.

In Siddle's research, his methodology included utilizing a **PRISim®** Video-Based Judgment Simulator, with a **ShootBack® Cannon**, installed in a trailer. Capable of firing a .68 caliber nylon ball at 120 feet per second, the officers' stress response was elevated, knowing the bad guy was actually able to shoot at them and hit them if they were not tactically sound. A single identical scenario was utilized for each officer, and a dispatcher was placed in the trailer to simulate real-time response and interaction. An air horn was sounded by a team member at a certain point during the scenario as well.

What distinguishes this work from others is that previous studies were never able to confirm whether survival stress had actually been induced, nor were researchers ever able to quantify the test subjects' actual performance against their perceived performance. Siddle therefore controlled as many environmental variables possible, and tracked physiological and cognitive changes as they occurred. He tracked heart rates, and by using blood samples, he measured changes in stress hormones and linked them to performance. He further had participants complete post-event surveys, and then compared them with real-time video playback of the subjects' performance.

The huge differentiator in Siddle's work is the blood analyses. It demonstrates, unequivocally, what happens to our Sympathetic Nervous System when we're exposed to a life-threatening event. A myriad of psycho-physiological effects occur, which include increased heart rate, adrenaline, and high levels of stress hormones, such as Cortisol, epinephrine, and norephinephrine. We also know that combat motor skills are affected, resulting in auditory exclusion and tunnel vision, to name just two. Siddle was joined by Dave Grossman in several studies involving combat-induced stress. The pair concluded that whenever a tremendous amount of stress is placed on the officer, there exists a huge potential for memory problems. They labeled this phenomenon, *Critical Incident Amnesia*. Siddle's research bears this out.

After the **PRISim®** scenario was complete, the officers were questioned about their performance. Comparing those responses to a review of the actual video produced a huge disparity between perceived performance and actual performance. The stress hormones increased, Cortisol an average of 18.15%, peaking as much as 206.41%. Epinephrine rose an average of 131.83%; norephinephrine an average of 66.26%. These high hormone levels impacted memory function.

To illustrate how increased levels of stress hormones can influence an officer's memory, Siddle asked each officer to describe their reaction to the threat on the screen. Half the participants responded that they saw the threat developing and reacted automatically. This was somewhat higher than the researchers believed to be true, based upon the researchers' observations. Researchers also felt that the number of officers who said they saw the threat develop but were slow to react, 38.1%, was slightly less than reported. Almost 12% of officers reported they were totally startled by the threat, but again, researches felt that number was almost double than the number reported.

The officers were queried regarding their initial response to the event. A large number, 88.10%, said they reacted based on their training. This number was much higher than the 66.67% indicated by the researchers. Surprisingly, while nearly 5% said their response to the scenario was fear, the researches felt that number was three times higher, at 16.67%.

Regarding auditory exclusion, recall that an air horn was sounded at some point during the scenario. The research indicated that almost 40% of the officers actually heard it and reacted to the stimulus, while 58% did not hear it. Those numbers are interesting, since a post-video survey question specifically asked if they heard any audio stimulus besides voice and weapon fire. The responses amounted to only 2.38% of participants who said they heard the air horn, even though almost 98% denied hearing the stimulus, many of them did, and either failed to realize it or forgot they heard it.

Data regarding the use of gun sights during the gunfight, indicated that only 30% of the officers reported being able to see their front sights. Of that number, only 25% reported actually using them. Researchers reviewing the footage indicated that 31.25% appeared to use their sights, which closely correlates to the participants' survey responses. Therefore, between 68-73% of the officers **did not use their sights** while engaged in the gun battle.

Findings with respect to the use of sights, begs the question: "How accurate are the officers when facing an adversary with a gun?" The obvious answer is not very accurate, and the officers' perception of their performance is quite disparate when compared to actual results. An average of 12.71 shots were fired per scenario; the rounds hit their mark an average of 3.3 times. The overall accuracy was computed to be 24.41%, which equates to one out of every four shots fired hits the bad guy. Of course, we're talking averages. Some of the officers hit almost 90% of their shots, yet others had no hits at all. A surprising 8% of officers failed to fire a single shot.

When asked about their shooting performance, the officers' perception exceeded the reality of what actually happened. Most felt they fired an average of 8.26 shots per scenario, and of those shots fired, 53% of them were felt to be accurate. The reality is 98% scored lower than their perception; 15% felt they hit the bad guy more times than they even fired. About 17% had no idea of how many rounds hit the bad guy. The most interesting statistic to be gleaned from the officers' memory of the shooting event is that only 12.90% correctly identified the number of rounds they fired during the scenario.

The above data, as well as the entire Siddle study, is a priceless resource for trainers. We need to endeavor to create the type of training that will maximize the limited time we have, to allow our officers to experience what they're likely to encounter on the street. It's been said that police work is hours of boredom, interspersed with moments of sheer terror. We need to train for those moments.

Links:
Bruce Siddle, Human Factor Research Group
http://www.hfrg.org/bruce-siddle/
Survival Stress Research and Post-Event Memory
http://findarticles.com/p/articles/mi_7745/is_200905/ai_n32424365/?tag=content;col1

SAY WHAT YOU MEAN AND MEAN WHAT YOU SAY

Words Have Meaning

I'm confused. I hear our politicians bemoaning the fact that our immigration problem is out of hand. Proposals for new legislation are bandied about in an effort to get a handle on what everyone admits is now a huge problem and getting larger each day. There is the usual political posturing; some pols are taking the moral high ground insisting that all of the undocumented immigrants are hardworking, law abiding, family types. I hear talk about amnesty programs that amount to allowing them all to stay as "guest workers" and after six years, they must return to their home country and wait in line to be obtain a visa and citizenship. What I don't hear is that these undocumented aliens are illegal. They have broken the law and are criminals and lawbreakers. Why are we so averse to calling them what they are?

Our present immigration laws address this problem very well. They state that if someone enters the United States illegally, the consequence is deportation. How difficult is that to understand and enforce, and why write more legislation when what we currently have is more than adequate? What is the purpose of calling an illegal alien an undocumented alien? Are we afraid of hurting law breakers' feelings? If that is the case, why then do we not call an auto thief an undocumented driver? He just does not have the required paperwork for that vehicle. Why do we not worry about his feelings? What about a bank robber. Should we refer to him as an undocumented bank customer? There are allegedly 12 million of these illegal aliens all over the country. What if there were the same amount of bank robbers on the loose—would there then be a hue and cry to grant them amnesty?

Words have meaning and when you take them out of context, they lose their intended meaning. "Undocumented" was never meant to mean "illegal." That was a product of the left and their attempt to avoid having  anyone feel uncomfortable. The only problem is that when no one feels uncomfortable, it means that no one has to earn anything. We have everyone expecting that they can achieve anything they desire, all they need to do is ask or apply. The correct noun to describe this situation is "entitlement." Entitlement is alive and well in our society. It is reflected in our laws, in our government policies and programs, and is firmly ensconced in our law enforcement academies.

Anyone that is involved in the vocation of training new recruits for police departments and law enforcement agencies will recognize the importance of saying what you mean and meaning what you say. Selection of individuals for recruit positions is rigorous. Criteria include background investigations, lie detector tests, and drug testing. The candidate is given the requirements for admission and knows what will be expected. Similarly, once chosen he or she knows what the curriculum consists of, as well as the testing standards. Why then do we see these standards not being adhered to across the board? Why do departments and agencies make exceptions to these measures of ability for certain individuals? Why do our academy directors not back the staff when a candidate is deemed unfit to be a member of that agency?

Is passing or failing based on one's own merits a radical idea? Is compelling a person to abide by established guidelines so far reaching that we must sometimes suspend the rules? The notion is ridiculous. Standards are a tried and true method of culling the herd. Just because one is accepted by a department doesn't mean that they automatically become a police officer. That honor must be earned. Recall a Marine motto: "Earned, Never Given." That should be the standard by which we measure our recruits. Just because a person excels in other aspects of training, does not mean that when they fail in another they should be given a pass. Words have meaning. Satisfying the curriculum means passing the tests as well—all of them. If one does not pass, he fails and is, appropriately, shown the door. We don't ignore the failure; we acknowledge it and thank them for their effort and desire.

Unfortunately, what I see becoming more prevalent is departments lowering the bar. In some cases I see the bar resting firmly on the ground, and I question those administrators as to why they even have a bar. The impression held by many of us in law enforcement is that some of our colleagues have not earned the right to wear the badge. We are aware of their marginal performance in training, which then becomes marginal on the street. Yet we hear from the powers that be that only the best and brightest comprise today's departments.

Words have meaning. The best and brightest conveys the best of the best. The best implies that someone is a cop because they earned that honor, not because they were entitled due to race, color, gender, family relationship, politics, or special skill. If that particular skill is important enough, allow that individual to be a non-sworn employee, a contractor, or a consultant for that department. Don't insult the other members and tarnish their efforts and sweat equity by suspending some of the same criteria that was successfully completed by everyone else. When you tell people that if requirements are not met, the result is dismissal, and then you fail to dismiss those individuals, you no longer mean what you say. Say what you mean and mean what you say.

SHOCKING KNIFE TRAINING!

Bringing Knife Training Up To Speed

A few quick statistics: 2% of all law enforcement officer assaults were with edged weapons; of that 2% assaulted, 14% suffered injuries, and seven officers were killed. These facts, culled over the past 10 years, are in the 2004 FBI Law Enforcement Officers Killed and Assaulted publication.

Less training is devoted to edged weapon defense than is devoted to firearms and tactics. I believe that one of the reasons for this is not only the number of firearms on the street, but also the perception that a gun is much more deadly than a knife. However, let us explore that misperception. I think that the officer should fear the knife more than he or she fears the gun. The reasons: a knife will generally result in a larger wound, there are no malfunctions with knives, accuracy with a knife is far better than with a gun, since point of aim is always point of impact, there is no reload needed with knives, and knives will penetrate officers' ballistic vests. Add into the mix that some officers are reluctant to even draw their gun when faced with an edged weapon, and you have the makings of a potential line of duty death.

So how do we train our officers to be better prepared when faced with an edged weapon attack? One way is to always include edged weapon training (EWT) as part of DTs, both for the newbie and in-service types. Training needs to be both dynamic and realistic. We have always had the dynamic portion covered, demonstrating blocks, knife attacks, and disarming techniques. However, the realistic aspect of training has been sorely lacking. Our training knives have typically been wooden and rubber knives. Trainees have mostly participated in the drills and techniques in a less than aggressive manner, since there has been no real consequence for them if they performed the block or disarming tactic incorrectly. The advent of the marking blade has helped, but that has a delayed evaluation and appears only after the drill is completed.

Approximately seven months ago, a new product, the Shocknife, was introduced into the law enforcement market. It has the ability to add a new dimension to EWT. The Shocknife, by virtue of its two 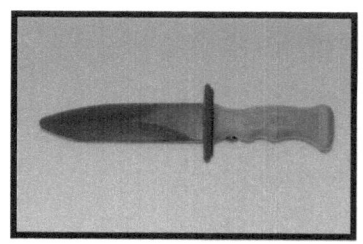 electrodes along the blade, delivers an immediate jolt to the trainee consisting of 7,500-volts. This sounds extreme, and indeed of the four settings: low, medium, high, and extreme, it would be was it not for the fact that the Shocknife delivers only .00075 amps at its highest setting. The result of this excellent training device is that the student receives immediate feedback on the technique performed. The trainee will feel as if he or she has actually been cut. Moreover, the sensation lingers for several minutes. The body is fooled into thinking that it has been cut and sends a pain stimulus to the brain. Having used the Shocknife myself, I can vouch for the immediate feeling of having been slashed.

Sgt. Jeff Quail of the Winnipeg Police Force in Canada developed the product out of the same frustration that many of us trainers feel when conducting EWT. Trainees fail to take the threat seriously; most of them half-heartedly walk through this block of instruction. Some display careless, even reckless behavior like grabbing at the knife blade, or picking the knife up by the blade rather than the handle. Introducing the Shocknife into EWT has added the element of realism that has been missing.

Quail reports that students now react with responses that are more appropriate: trainees back up rather than grab for the blade; students draw their weapon, create space, and attempt to put an obstacle between the threat and themselves. At its highest setting, extreme, the Shocknife sparks and growls. This feature induces "acute stress," equating the fear of being shocked with the fear of being cut. This is truly reality-based training.

I spoke with FBI Special Agent Ray Flannagan about the Shocknife. Ray teaches DTs at the FBI Academy in Quantico, VA. He told me that they are in the process of evaluating the Shocknife, and he feels that it is an excellent tool, especially for specialized units and scenario-based training. "The Shocknife elicits fear in the trainee just like a real knife would," Flanagan said. He added, "Having a pain response adds the element of realism that gives value to our training." Flannagan's colleague, Special Agent Butch Greathouse, echoed the same sentiments and said that he is a huge proponent of anything that adds realism to training, "That's what ultimately keeps our people alive," he said.

Heretofore, the best way to demonstrate that facing an edged weapon was a deadly force situation was the 21-Foot Rule, developed by Salt Lake City trainer Dennis Tueller over 20 years ago. Now that the Shocknife has been invented, my sense is that there will be fewer officers injured and killed from edged weapon attacks.

SHOTS FIRED FOURTH FLOOR

Are you working a one-man unit in a two-man car?

The lookout message said we were looking for a white male subject, early 20s, wearing a white tee shirt, blue jeans, and high top sneakers. We passed by the alley and caught a glimpse of a possible suspect running into a yard. My partner quickly aimed our squad in that direction and we both jumped out in pursuit. He had a jump on us, his white shirt appearing briefly on the first floor landing of a back porch staircase of a four story apartment building. We shouted, "Police, Stop!" The warnings had no effect, as is most always the case.

My partner and I raced up the first flight, a rush of adrenaline surging through our bodies. By the second flight of stairs, my partner's non-existent physical fitness program had left him gasping for air, hardly able to continue. However, I was in high gear reaching the third flight simultaneous to our bad guy making it to the top floor.

Stopping at the back door to listen, I heard some noise from inside and quickly surveyed what I now realized was another abandoned structure. Looking around what was once the kitchen, I saw syringes and other drug paraphernalia lying on the floor. I surmised that the guy I'm chasing may know the layout of this flophouse and have an even greater advantage on me.

I wanted to grab this guy as quickly as possible, and not give him time to hunker down while I made my way inside. I heard my partner still laboring as he walked up several steps trying to join me. I was on my own, armed with only my street smarts, training, and St. Michael as my backup.

I quick-peeked my way into the next room and found nothing but debris and feces on the floor. No danger areas here; I made my way to the next opening where I stopped and listened. I heard him—the breathing—he's in here I thought. I sliced the pie and saw a darkened room with just a few pieces of furniture. Good I thought; darkness is my friend. I pulled a light from the pouch on my belt and quickly lit the room by bouncing the beam off the ceiling. He's there—over in the corner—an alcove that must have once served as a shelving unit; I saw his shoulder. Just inside the room and off to my left, stood an old armoire. That would be my cover. I strobed my light in the direction of the alcove, shouting, "Police, Come Out!" At the same time, I dashed to my point of cover.

As I made it to the bulky piece of furniture, two shots rang out from the corner in the direction of my last position. My bad guy's muzzle flash allowed me to get a perfect fix on his position. I returned fire, the blast illuminating my target perfectly. I heard him drop; he immediately began to moan and cry for help. I set my light on the floor to illuminate him and moved my position. Pulling out my second light, I was ready to blind him once again, but I could see his gun several feet from him. It was obvious that he had given up the fight.

Shaken from both the steep ascent and the sound of gunfire, my partner finally joined me as I made my way forward to cuff our suspect. We quickly got him under control, retrieved his weapon, and looked for additional weapons and anyone else that might be in the apartment. Score one for the good guys…training had allowed this one to end with a good outcome.

The above account is fictional, but nonetheless, it's taken from personal experience and accounts from colleagues over the course of 33 years of police work. This short story illustrates several points that emphasize the importance of training in our job.

Physical fitness training allowed our fictional officer to chase the suspect up four flights of stairs without any problem; it further allowed him to control himself physiologically during a time of extreme danger. His fitness gave him the ability to instantly formulate a plan, and then implement that plan. His heartbeat was under control, and he was focused on his target. By being in shape, his mind was clear and his actions were crisp and forceful. He presented an overwhelming presence to his adversary.

Our officer's tactical training and firearms skills allowed him to quickly dominate the situation and end it quickly. His knowledge of low light tactics, movement, and use of cover, made him a skilled warrior that quickly demoralized his opponent and gave him no options or openings to inflict harm on the officer.

So what was our officer's Achilles Heel? You guessed it...his partner. Even though his colleague may have had skills equal to those of his partner, they all become useless when he was not able to stand by his side and utilize them. The officer's poor physical conditioning effectively reduced that two man unit to "one man" status. The poorly conditioned officer then became a liability rather than an asset.

So I ask you...are you lacking in any area? Could your firearms skills, tactics, or physical conditioning be improved? Is so, why aren't you aggressively working to bring whatever skill that you are deficient in up to speed. What are you waiting for? Be proactive. Take inventory of yourself, and as painful as it may be, admit that you need work in one of those areas and then get on it. You will be a better person and a better cop. It may just save your life or mine one day.

SPRAY TODAY, GONE TOMORROW.

Is pepper spray obsolete?

With the introduction of the Taser® most officers are finding that open space on their belt is a limited commodity. A large number of officers have the ability to carry three intermediate level weapons: the baton, OC spray and Taser®. However, with their duty belts maxed out and heavier than ever, officers are questioning whether they still need to carry OC spray. Many believe that the Taser® is a suitable replacement option for OC. This article will explore the benefits of carrying all three less-lethal options, as well as explain the tactical benefits that OC spray can provide that other weapons cannot.

Contrary to early marketing campaigns, officers must recognize that OC spray was not designed to "physically" incapacitate resistant subjects. Rather, the original intent was to give officers a tactical advantage by possibly "psychologically" incapacitating the subject. The tactical advantage is gained by restricting the vision, restricting respiration depth, and potentially causing an inward focus on pain.

The difference between physical incapacitation and psychological incapacitation is defined as follows: psychological incapacitation describes the inability to provide physical resistance regardless of the will or conscious decision to resist. Non-compliant subjects consciously chose to focus on the pain and stop resisting, instead of making a conscious decision to accept the pain and continue fighting. True physical incapacitation involves the inability to resist, regardless of the mental will of the individual. When an officer chooses to deploy OC spray on a resistant subject, his mindset should be one in which he recognizes that it will give him a tactical advantage over his adversary. If the subject stops resisting as a result of the spray, the officer should view this as a bonus—never as the singular result of opting to spray. And, if the only result of spraying a subject is that he has a choice whether or not to focus on the pain and give up, then of what benefit is OC spray? This is where an understanding of the actual design of OC spray illustrates why it is an essential weapon for officers to continue to carry on the street. By understanding that OC spray is designed to give an officer a tactical advantage by restricting vision, restricting breath depth, and introducing pain, several advantages are realized.

First, the ability to restrict the vision of the subject provides a huge tactical advantage to officers. Vision is the most important sense to a human involved in a physical altercation. Vision allows an assailant to locate the officer and quickly obtain target acquisition for any technique or tactic. The ability for an officer to take away acquisition ability will provide an edge to that officer.

Second, the ability to restrict the depth of the breath provides a tactical advantage by reducing the ability to acquire advanced respiration. When involved in a physical altercation or fleeing from officers, an assailant will require a greater level of oxygen exchange to assist in performance. This is usually performed by having deeper respiration. Once OC particles enter the lungs, the ability to take deep breaths is hampered.

Third, the pain caused by contact on the skin, and particle inhalation, may compel a subject to mentally focus on that sensation. Again, officers must understand that this is a conscious decision made by the offender. But even if the offender does not choose to stop resisting, the pain can constantly interfere with their thought process. This can slow down their decision-making abilities, allowing officers to capitalize on the break in mental focus.

Finally, here are five reasons why OC spray is unique and valuable as an intermediate weapon and why it should continue to be carried by officers:

FIRST: OC spray can be utilized on multiple, resistant subjects from a distance. The delivery system of OC spray allows for quick application of the product to several individuals at once. If the officer has a fogging spray or stream, this type of application becomes even easier. Unfortunately, Taser® can only be realistically used on one subject at a time.

SECOND: OC spray does not rely on the size, strength and physical abilities of the officer. A baton is more effective in the hands of the larger, stronger, and more skilled officer. The strength and effectiveness of the application of OC spray will always be the same regardless of what officer applies the product. Unlike multiple baton strikes that require physical exertion, OC spray will not tax the officers physically.

THIRD: OC spray can be used to motivate movement of an assailant from a physical area. If a subject is found hiding in a concealed area and refuses to comply with demands to come out, officers can contaminate the area without having to expose themselves to potential danger. This can be done by either utilizing a spray or one of the new OC expulsion grenades that are safe and flameless.

FOURTH: OC is small, light and cheap. The MK-3 canisters are small in size but carry multiple burst capacity. They are not heavy like batons, and are far less costly than replacement cartridges for the Taser®.

FIFTH: OC requires minimal training. I have often informed my students that if I tossed a couple of canisters into the monkey cage at our local zoo, within five minutes they would be spraying each other. The weapon is a very simple tool to operate. After covering safety and decontamination, the bulk of the training should be centered around when and how to use the product to get maximum tactical advantage.

Comparisons between Taser® and OC spray are like comparing apples and oranges. Tasers® are designed to physically incapacitate a resistant subject, whereas OC spray is designed to provide a tactical advantage to officers. As you can see, the tactical advantages that OC spray can provide are substantial. The key is for officers to be properly trained to understand what OC spray can offer them when confronted with a non-compliant subject. If you recognize that incapacitation is not the primary intent for OC spray, then you understand that the tactical advantage it can provide you with is valuable. I hope that those of you that have removed this important less lethal tool from your duty belt and placed it in your duffle bag will get that holster back on your belt where it belongs.

__Jeff Quail__ is the inventor of ShocKnife and co-authored this article. Jeff is currently a Sergeant with a major municipal Canadian Police Service. He has 16 years' experience. Jeff has several Instructor Trainer and Instructor level certifications in the area of officer safety, defensive tactics and firearms.

STREET SURVIVAL

Show me the money

I've been teaching and writing about Street Survival for years. Generally when we mention the concept, everyone knows what we're talking about—surviving physical encounters on the street. But I submit to you that there is another type of "Street Survival," one that doesn't get much attention. What I'm referring to is surviving the temptations on the street that cops all over the nation face each day. How does one survive them, and what type of training is required? Let's take a look at the ethical minefield that we have to navigate during the course of our duties.

There is an often used misquoted phrase, "money is the root of all evil." The actual quote has its roots in the New Testament and actually reads, "For the love of money is the root of all evil…" Regardless of which phrase is used, they both have the same meaning—money, or the lack of it, can be problematic and compel us to act out of character. Think about the times that you may have come upon a situation where you have had individuals gambling on a street corner or maybe on the stoop of a business. When they see the cops pull up, most times everyone scatters in different directions. Once in a while, one of the participants may scoop up the money. But more often than not it's left behind on the sidewalk.

Now comes the time when your character becomes challenged; your morals are tested. What's to be done with that pot of money that no one cares to claim as their own? We all know that the right thing to do is to fill out a report and inventory it as found property. But what happens when there happens to be a substantial amount, say several hundred dollars, enough to make a car payment or buy groceries for a week. Do you hesitate...look around to see who may be watching? Do you collect it and still go into the station to file a report, but only inventory half of the money? If you're a one-man unit, it becomes even easier.

How about the drug bust where you wind up tossing someone on the street and come up with a wad of cash and a stash of dope? It would be simple to tell the guy to take a hike, and pocket the money. The same temptation presents itself on drug raids, where stacks of cash and large amounts of drugs are found. When you're dealing with thousands of dollars, it would be easy to tuck a few hundred dollars in your pocket.

You make a traffic stop in which the driver is on probation, doesn't have a license, or any number of things that may cause him to offer you some money to send him on his way. Who would know? Certainly the driver isn't going to rat you out, and if you're working alone it would be fairly easy to make it happen. Who couldn't use a hundred bucks? Sometimes it's not even money that becomes hard to refuse. Remember pulling over that blond in the red car, wearing the too short skirt that seemed to ride up higher each time she implied that you wouldn't regret not writing her a ticket?

The list is endless. The temptations strike a chord in some form or fashion with all of us. Maybe it's the cop in a rural county that has a tough time supporting his wife and five kids on a salary that is way below the national norm. Or the cop who may be in over his head with bills from a spouse with a substance abuse problem. It could be any number of factors that cause one of us to hesitate and think about taking that money, or accepting that favor.

Unfortunately some of our colleagues have been tempted and have taken the bait. I'm sure that afterward the shame and regret was overwhelming. And after you've done it once, what's to prevent you from continuing to take even more money? I'm sure the rationale is, "I've already broken the law, how can it get any worse?"

But I submit to you that it can and will get a whole lot worse. Once you accept a certain type of behavior as "the norm," it becomes easier to act in the same manner. The first time you take something it may be traumatic, even though you rationalize in your mind that it's drug money and doesn't really belong to anyone. The next time an opportunity to take money or goods presents itself, it's easier to do—not much thought is given to the morality of the act. It becomes easier and easier, and maybe you even justify it by convincing yourself that you actually deserve the money because you work so hard and constantly put yourself in harm's way.

Once you lose your moral compass, it's very difficult to find your way back. What becomes inevitable is that you will eventually be discovered and your career will be over. If you're lucky you may avoid going to jail. But besides the dream job and pension that you've lost, the more important thing that you no longer have is your reputation. It takes years and years to build a good, moral character. As we watch the Presidential election unfold, we constantly hear the word "character" being used, especially in the phrase: "Character counts."

There is a quote attributed to an individual named Frank Outlaw that says, "Watch your thoughts; they become words. Watch your words; they become actions. Watch your actions;

they become habits. Watch your habits; they become character. Watch your character; it becomes your destiny."

Those are indeed words to live by. When you become a cop, you automatically become a respected member of society. You are held in high esteem, indeed, little children look up to you as a hero. Don't let them down, and more importantly, don't let yourself down. If you face a moral or ethical dilemma, simply ask yourself, "What would my family think of the decision that I'm about to make?" You can't go wrong if you use that standard. Say your prayers and treat everyone like you would want to be treated.

THE UNSPEAKABLE HORROR

"The thought of suicide is a great source of comfort; with it a calm passage is to be made across many a bad night."

That quote by German Philosopher Friedrich Nietzsche may explain the actions taken by a Chicago police officer just a couple of weeks ago. Upset about his divorce and in a fit of depression, he committed an unspeakable act—he shot his two children. His beautiful seven-year-old daughter died from a gunshot to the head; his little nine-year-old son is in critical condition from his head wound. The officer then took his own life. He was discovered by fellow officers, lying dead from a self-inflicted gunshot to the head.

If you've ever answered a call like this, one in which a fellow officer has committed suicide or a murder/suicide, it's an image that is indelibly etched in your mind. It lingers, it haunts, it demonizes your psyche, and it causes you to question your faith. You will never forget that scene, indeed it will become like a cancer eating away at your very core until you are forced to do something to either erase it, or at least minimize its impact on you. Some officers go down the wrong road; they turn to things like alcohol or drugs. They feel compelled to "blot it out," to "numb" those painful recollections of an event too painful even to talk about.

Yet that's exactly what needs to be done—to talk about it. Too often, we as cops put that "macho cop" image out there for everyone to see. We build that wall around us, fearful of anything that might make us remember the horror. And I'm talking about both guys and gals. Our sisters behind the badge see glimpses of hell as often as their male counterparts. No one is immune to the after effects of a critical incident like the suicide of a co-worker. To be involved in any way in a case like this, whether it's recovery of the body, as a negotiator, or even a dispatcher as my fellow writer Michelle Perin points out in an earlier article, leaves a hole in one's soul. That damage needs to be repaired quickly before it leads to a total change of one's own identity.

My 33 years in law enforcement brought me close to several suicides. They are one of our dirty little secrets—not many people realize how pervasive the problem is. The National Police Suicide Foundation states that an average of 450 law enforcement suicides have taken place in the last three years, yet only 2% of LE agencies have prevention programs to combat the problem. I can recall that during my tenure with the FBI, there were years when we saw the number of agent deaths by suicide larger than line of duty deaths. And whether you're a federal agent or a police officer the availability of that gun is the commonality—it's always there; it's a part of you. It makes the act of killing one's self quick and easy. We've been trained to take a life if we must, and we are confident that we can take our own—if we choose to.

However, what can possibly be so bad; what depth of

despair must be reached when the only answer is to end one's life? How can we not have at least one small sliver of light shining onto our otherwise blackened, uncaring soul? What causes us to sink below the water and not fight to capture that life-saving breath of air? The pragmatic answer is that there is no circumstance that will justify taking that drastic step. But we're human beings and many of us allow our emotions to control our actions. In the heat of the moment we've all done things that we later regret, said things that we're ashamed to have said. But suicide…?

I certainly do not have all the answers for the tragedy in Chicago, nor will I pass judgment on the actions that took place there. My prayers are for the babies and for the officer, and my faith tells me that God is a compassionate God. That's where I seek my comfort. But my question is this: Could it have been avoided?

According to the experts—maybe. The warning signs are usually evident: heavy drinking, a strained marriage, separation, divorce, erratic behavior, they're all visible manifestations of inner turmoil. There's a silent cry for help that needs to be answered in the form of peer counseling, professional counseling, or just a one on one talk with a partner or close friend. To dismiss the signs is to add fuel to the fire; it's not going to burn itself out. It needs to be laid out on the table, not put away in the drawer.

Intervention is necessary, and simply saying "it's going to be okay" isn't going to help. I can guarantee that most times the effort to interject yourself into that person's life will be resisted. As a former EAP Peer Counselor, I've seen it. No one likes to admit to weakness, addiction, or personal problems of any type—especially cops. We're supposed to be tough; we're immune to the horrors that would cause a normal person to faint or to flee. However, try as we may to inoculate ourselves to these horrific events, we never seem to have the right dosage. We're always just on the edge of being able to totally turn off our human emotions.

And while we need to shine the spotlight on prevention, we also need to shed light on the survivors of suicide—the one's left behind. Those left in the wake of a disaster like the one in Chicago, need caring for; the emergency personnel, the cops, the dispatchers, crime scene people, the hospital ER, even the coroner who deals with death each day—they all need to talk. These horrific events can have a devastating impact on someone already on the verge of developing psychological problems. To leave a vivid image unchecked may just be the trigger that sets someone into a downward spiral.

Comfort and compassion are the keys, not silence and denial. To my brothers and sisters out there I urge you to talk about this sad event. Unfortunately, this is a dangerous part of our job, not unlike facing down a gunman. This is reality; this can happen to any one of us unless we're proactive and have the fortitude to face it head on. Reassuring your colleagues that sadness, tears, and other emotions are all normal is the key to mental fitness. To hold everything inside, sometimes for years, can lead to grief, depression, anxiety, and even withdrawal from friends and family. We need each other, and in times such as these it becomes even more critical that we look out for each other. I urge you to pray for Chicago Police Officer Dannie Marchan and his family. God bless you.

THE CAPITAL OFFENSE

Not training the way you fight.

We've all seem them: officers quick to explain that the reason they didn't complete a task or event properly is because it wasn't real. The usual retort: "If this were a real incident, I would have handled it differently." Would they? You and I as trainers know the answer to that question: **The way you train is the way you fight.** How many times have you heard that adage, or for that matter, how often do you use it?

What are some of the other excuses for poor performance?

- Lack of knowledge and ability
- Pressure resulting from performing in front of peers
- Apathy—not caring about training, being there because you have to attend

If you are like me, you have probably used that phrase, **the way you train is the way you fight,** countless times to counter those training skeptics. The idea that an individual that trains differently than the way they operate on the street, and then expects different results, is sheer lunacy. To expect that you will perform your duties and react appropriately to threats is just not going to happen. Let's explore why.

In terms of preparing yourself for police work, there are two points of reference that we use as our compass: experience and training.

We combine those two components of the equation to give

us our result. Those of us with many years of experience have a wealth of knowledge to draw upon; conversely those with little have less. Regardless of whichever category you may fall under, the other half of the equation is training. Both officers need to bolster their experience with training. The training should be both meaningful and redundant. Why redundant? Because we know that training that is repetitive gives us the ability to store that tactic, that move, or that task into our short-term memory. Why do we want it in short-term memory versus long-term? Simply because short-term memory allows us to access the information needed more quickly. If we can get to the information that we need quickly, that allows us to cut down on our reaction time. In a critical incident, quick reaction often translates into survival.

Think of short-term and long-term memory this way. Picture your brain as being a file cabinet. All of our memories are stored in that file cabinet/brain. When we need to access things that haven't happened in a long time, i.e. long-term memory, it causes us to look to the back of the drawer. It takes time to look through many files and papers. Contrast that to information stored in front of the drawer, which is short-term memory, that information is quickly accessible. An example of long-term memory might be your friend who sat behind you in school in the third grade. That takes us a while to remember, it's not something that we often think about. Now, think about driving your car. Most of the time you operate your vehicle without even thinking about what you are doing. Stepping on the gas or the brake takes hardly any thought process at all because you do it repetitively. That is an example of short-term memory. That illustrates the value of training. If we train often enough, doing the same things repeatedly, they are stored in the short-term memory. Those acts or tactics then become instinctual, you don't even think about doing them, you do them automatically. Again, accessing information in short-term memory affords us quicker reaction time.

Why am I concerned about quick reaction? Well, let's discuss a principle that I hope all of us are familiar with: **Action vs. Reaction**. Simply put, action beats reaction every time. The best we can hope for in law enforcement is a tie. Is a tie a satisfactory outcome, especially in a gunfight? No. Therefore, our goal is to reduce our reaction time as much as possible, to at least put us on a level playing field with the bad guys. Police work, being mostly reactive, means that the more we decrease our reaction time, the better chance we have of surviving a critical incident. We know that the quickest reaction times are between a quarter second and a half-second, and that is usually found in well-trained athletes. Our reaction time will generally be close to that, but only if we are well trained ourselves. There again lies the value of repetitive training.

Not training the way that you fight causes confusion. There is no clear course of action to follow, since we train one way and fight another. The brain is confused, our reaction slowed, and our performance poor. Poor performance is, for the most part, inconsequential in training, but poor performance can be disastrous on the street. Successful, repetitive training results in self-confidence. When you are confident in your skills and abilities, your capacity to face challenges and survive critical incidents, meaning your ability to survive, increases exponentially.

By way of reinforcing our axiom, **the way you train is the way you fight,** let me relate an incident. Several years ago, I was involved in teaching street survival courses to FBI Violent Crime Task Forces. The weeklong training involved what you would normally expect: lectures on "The Psyche of Survival", tactics, vehicle stops, room clearing, etc. Shortly after completing instruction for a task force out of the New York area, my colleagues and I received an email from one of the former students. He had been involved in serving a warrant on a violent fugitive. During the course of the arrest, which took place in a hotel lobby, the subject was non-compliant and drew a weapon. Without hesitation, the student's recent training "kicked in automatically" and caused him to react instinctually. The result was that the agent was unharmed when the bad guy drew a weapon. The fugitive was not so lucky. He emphasized to us that without the training he doesn't think that he would have survived the incident—which naturally reinforced what we already knew. That's why I call it the Capital Offense, since: **The way you train is the way you fight!** To think otherwise is a *possible death sentence.*

THE DIRTY LITTLE SECRET

The constant refrain that I hear is that the poor, hard-working illegals are doing the jobs that Americans refuse to do. To begin with,, that lie was disabused when scores of illegal immigrants (1,262 to be exact) were arrested in December 2006 at the Swift & Company meat plants across six states. Immediately following their removal by federal agents, job applicants (American citizens) lined up around the block applying for positions to replace the politically correct (PC) labeled "undocumented workers." Why? Because contrary to public opinion, the illegals were working well-paying jobs that Americans are willing to work! Swift pays the illegals more than minimum wage, but does not offer them any benefits.

In this way costs are kept at a minimum, and the employees know not to make any waves or display any sign of displeasure or they will be out of a job. This begs the question: why were none of the Swift management execs arrested for allowing these folks to work? Why is there no consequence when the company doing the hiring blatantly breaks the law? The easy answer is that the arrest of any company executive would not fit the PC template. To add insult to injury, forged documents and identity theft were commonplace amidst the hiring practices.

ID theft and forgery are bad enough, but now here is the **"dirty little secret"** that no one will tell you about--our beloved illegals, the folks that our legislators refer to as good, family-oriented people and the backbone of America, are **sex fiends**! There are approximately 240,000 illegal immigrant sex offenders in the U.S. This according to Andy Selepak, in an article written for *The Family Security Foundation, Inc.*, on January 10, 2007.These predators have victimized nearly one million of us, perpetrating crimes including rape, child molestation, sexual homicides, and rape and molestation of handicapped children. Why is it that we never hear about U.S. citizens victimized by illegals? Once again, the simple answer is that it simply does not fit the PC template. An unbelievable 93 sex offenders illegally cross the border each day. Are our legislators concerned? Don't make me laugh. The new Congress is now re-evaluating the very need for a border fence. This after the voters demanded a fence built--so much for your vote meaning anything to a politician.

In Los Angeles, 95 percent of all outstanding warrants for homicide (which totaled 1,200 to 1,500) in the first half of 2004, targeted illegal aliens. Up to two-thirds of all fugitive felony warrants (17,000) were for illegal aliens. This information was gleaned from testimony on April 13, 2005, given by Heather MacDonald, Senior Fellow, Manhattan Institute for Policy Research, before the House Judiciary Subcommittee on Immigration, Border Security, and Claims. Miss MacDonald spoke about "sanctuary laws," which basically prevent law enforcement officers from inquiring about the citizenship of an individual and reporting it to federal authorities. You guys and gals on the street know exactly what I am talking about. Heaven forbid the local news media gets their hands on a story about you making a field stop and determining that your subject is in the country illegally. MacDonald emphasizes that these sanctuary laws "place a higher priority on protecting illegal aliens from deportation than on protecting legal immigrants and citizens from assault, rape, arson, and other crimes."

MacDonald's testimony further illustrated how these outlaw illegals survive, especially in California. Most of the gangs consist of illegal immigrants that thrive on violence, drug dealing, and intimidation. The notorious "Mara Salvatrucha" gang is said to be overwhelmingly illegal. Our police departments and federal agencies know this to be true, yet our Congress continues to take the position that these are hard-working people that are only trying to feed their families.

Why do we tolerate these sanctuary laws? The basic premise is that the illegals will be encouraged to work with the authorities. That is laughable. One would need to dig deep to find an instance where an illegal immigrant provided any solid evidence to the police regarding another illegal. Moreover, most illegals are not even aware of these ridiculous laws and could care less. Whenever an alien is apprehended and a deportation order carried out, most times we find the offender back in the U.S. quicker than the piece of paper can be filed away. Take a look at their criminal histories to find that many of the heinous crimes these cretins commit occur after they have re-entered the country subsequent to being deported.

The above numbers should make all of us shudder in fear and disbelief, but more importantly make you question why the do-nothing Congress continues to ignore the problem that, frankly, is killing us! Some true Americans continue to fight. In Hazelton, PA, the new Republican mayor has enacted new laws that make English the official language in his town. He also had laws passed that make the employers that hire the illegals responsible for their actions. The ACLU and Hispanic activist groups are fighting the mayor in court, but Hazelton's message has had an impact. Roughly 30 percent of the town's Hispanics have moved out. In March, Hazelton will defend the new ordinances in court. Too bad, it seems not only are we being victimized on the street by the illegals, but we have to battle them in our courts as well—even though we are U.S. citizens and they are not. Thanks Congress, keep up the good work.

THE GIFT

The month of December is one of the more difficult times of the year for many people. It's rife with trepidation about the holidays. Parents wonder if they'll be able to fulfill their children's wishes for gifts to place underneath the Christmas tree, while the children themselves secretly hope that Santa will grant their requests for the latest toys they've seen advertised since summer.

Those of us in law enforcement face our own special challenges during this unique time of year. Many of us will be working Christmas Eve and/or Christmas. We accept it as part of the job, but that does not diminish the stress that being away from our loved ones always creates. We miss many family moments, ones we can never get back or recreate. Moreover, during the course of our tour on the holiday, we are exposed to unfortunates who suffer tragedy and sorrow on the very day that should fill them with joy and feelings of good will.

Having endured holiday work schedules many times, I can offer some advice concerning the perfect gift to give your family. Over the years I've witnessed my colleagues fret over what presents to get their loved ones. They've stressed over jewelry for their spouse, each year a different piece is in vogue, tennis bracelets one year, diamond earrings the next. The children have their status piece to acquire as well, that special toy or tech gadget that every child must have. I recall in the past some of the must-have novelties included oddball items such as Cabbage Patch dolls and Tickle Me Elmo. A year later, many of the formerly treasured toys took center stage at garage sales.

Often, my co-workers were obsessed with getting popular items any way possible, to the point of calling department stores, reading every sale paper, and even answering personal ads placed by unscrupulous people who sell hard to find treasures at ridiculously inflated prices. No matter, my colleagues were pay prepared to pay any price, they had to have them.

Over the years, I've seen lines of people crisscrossing department store parking lots at one o'clock in the morning, in snow, rain, and freezing temperatures, waiting for the opportunity to buy that one special gift. It stands to reason that there is a limit to how many items a store can carry in its inventory, whether it's flat screen televisions, laptop computers, talking dolls, or Play Stations. Someone is going to be disappointed and go home empty handed.

Invariably, whenever anxious people crowd together, disagreements develop, pushing and shoving ensues, and frustration with not getting the reward for their time and effort manifests itself in the form of slugfests and threats. The police are eventually called, and what began innocently as a quest to please a loved one, turns into a nightmare resulting in a parent going to jail. Sad. What's even sadder is that we are the ones tasked with maintaining order and arresting those offenders who cross the line, all the while knowing that their original intent was a genuine love for their children and an attempt to please them. Stress.

Another situation always encountered during the Christmas holidays, is the call from a family who arrives home and finds all of their presents stolen. Burglaries during the holidays are heart-breaking. I can't decide which is worse, the abject depression of the parents who toiled long and hard to buy the gifts, or the look of despair on the children's faces who know that this year the toy cupboard will be bare.

These incidents cause more stress for LEOs, borne out of a feeling of helplessness and anger. It's difficult to maintain one's sanity and compassion in the face of so much evil. The easy answer is to turn to something that eases the pain. That soft place to land often times comes in the form of alcohol, drugs, or someone who seems to care and wants to listen.

Holidays are a magical time for many, but for others they can be times when we let our guard down and succumb to temptation. That invitation to stop for a drink after work, or the party you're called to break up which results in a good looking party goer inviting you to have a drink with them after your shift, has the potential to lead to disaster. It takes a strong person to say no to such enticing situations, and unless you are an individual with a strong moral code, you will likely succumb.

This is where the "the gift" comes in, one that your family will treasure for a lifetime. I'm not referring to a tangible gift, one of jewelry or electronics, toys or clothing. Rather, I'm referring to something intangible, something that you may not regularly give. That something, that gift, is YOU.

Think about this for a moment. What's the one thing your spouse and/or children always ask? If you're like most of us, the answer is: "When are you coming home?" Your family, more than anything else, wants you to be with them, they want time with the one person they cherish more than any bracelet or doll—they want their mom and dad, their husband or wife. Giving the gift of you is priceless. And if you've ever been injured on duty—shot, stabbed, beaten, involved in a serious car accident—you may have been nudged already by your Creator to do just that.

Those of you who haven't been given the wakeup call, nevertheless, need to hear the message. It's very simple. Don't leave your home without hugging your loved ones and telling them you love them—say the words. Don't leave with a problem or argument unresolved. Remember to tell your family members that you value them above all else. Get your priorities in order: Faith, Family, Job; everything else is secondary. Always remember this*: **To the world you are but one person, but to one person you are the world.** Don't disappoint the very people who want nothing more than the gift of YOU.

Merry Christmas, brothers and sisters!

THE POLITICS OF KILLING

Getting shot with paper bullets

On any given day, in any city across this great nation of ours, one can read a headline emblazoned across a local newspaper containing words similar to these: "Cops Shoot Man Who Has Toy Gun," or perhaps, "Unarmed College Student Killed by Cops." Recently, we were reminded by the press about how murderous we cops really are, vis-a-vis the Sean Bell case. In particular, the New York papers reported, with what seemed to be a sense of glee, that Mr. Bell had been killed in a hail of 50 bullets.

Whenever we read reports such as the ones mentioned above that are purported to be factual, we never hear much about what prompted the cops to use deadly force. Moreover, most victims of police shootings are eerily cut from the same cloth—they were minding their own business, they were respected members of their community, they were loved by everyone, they were hard-working, and none of them had ever said a bad word about anyone. Sound familiar?

The news media sink their collective teeth into police shooting stories, especially if the cops are white and the individual killed was black. Racism, or the mere hint of it, sells papers. Circumstances and justification rarely factor into reportage. No doubt you've heard the old axiom, "If it bleeds it leads." Any police incident in which cops have fired their weapons is front page news more often than not. I have no qualms about the media reporting incidents involving police gunfire. Indeed, all of us as citizens expect that the news media will report the events that shape our communities every day. What seems remarkable however is that most shootings that are reported are couched in terms of the police having done something untoward.

The manner in which many of the shooting occurrences are reported, seem to insinuate that the cops were wrong, or that they were covering something up. This unethical, and often times inflammatory reporting, only serves as kindling to ignite a bonfire of hatred and mistrust by demagogues who purport to be spiritual or civic leaders of the community. It causes one to think that perhaps the media is in a partnership with hate-mongers, and those that would stir up emotions to the point of civil unrest.

The ethics question that immediately comes to my mind is this, "How does a reporter justify not reporting a story in-depth, i.e., only covering the side of the alleged victim, and. not fully investigating the police explanation of what occurred?" How does that qualify as a fair and balanced analysis—an unbiased account? The quick answer is that unless they frame the story in terms of a "defenseless, innocent victim," the story has no legs.

The other aspect of how the media shoots us with their "paper bullets," is how many people think about the mechanics of killing. To the extent that the television and movies have portrayed unrealistic expectations of shootings, i.e., the ability to shoot a weapon from someone's hand, or "Dirty Harry" killing someone with one round that blows that individual through a plate glass window, the media, just like a few of us, expect that police can wound or kill somebody with one well-placed round. When that fails to happen in the real world, when someone continues to fight even though struck several times with what proves later to be lethal rounds, the media jumps all over the authorities demanding an explanation. Yet, when for whatever reason, the police fail to use deadly force, or in the instance of an active shooter, they fail to move on the shooter immediately, the media are quick to assign blame for cops' reluctance to act.

In terms of the ethical responsibility involved in reporting and documenting deadly force situations, I not only fault the press, but contend that our own departments share the blame as well. We are reluctant to hold the media's feet to the fire. When bad reporting happens, we need to get out in front of the cameras and set the record straight. Police work just doesn't happen on the street; police work involves every aspect of the job. Just as we advise the people we serve in matters of legalities, so also must we advise the social structure that surrounds our community. The cops that hold admin positions are still sworn to back us up when the need arises. If that means addressing cases of media inaccuracies, then our own media reps need to have our backs. If we allow the press to continue down the path of sensationalism without stopping them, then we unwittingly sanction all that they say and do.

As a writer, I have an obligation to report *all* of the facts surrounding a story, not just those that I cherry pick. In prosecutions, to withhold any exculpatory evidence is unethical behavior as well. Just as we are expected to adhere to the highest of standards, we should also demand that our media operate within those same parameters. When they do not, we need to be proactive in our effort to "reboot' the reporting process to get it back in sync with reality.

THE REAL YOU

It's not who you see in the mirror.

You get out of the shower and admire yourself in the mirror as you dry off. Suck in that stomach, puff up that chest, and flex those arms—man, what a specimen! I think that all of us, at one time, have done this in the past. We like to think that we are in good shape, that maybe we even resemble one of the pro athletes or bodybuilders that we see on television, in magazines, or at the movies. We can make that person in the mirror more than what he or she actually is, and really believe it! However, is that who we really are?

We sometimes have a tendency to lose touch with reality, especially if nothing has recently happened that "snaps us back in," so to speak. We go along doing the same things the same way without any repercussions or serious consequences. We are lulled into a false sense of security, thinking that we really have our act together—that we are operating on all cylinders and with the utmost efficiency. But are we really, or are we just lucky that the challenges that we have faced up to this point have been relatively simple and within our comfort zone?

Let's talk about training for a moment, particularly physical training. What are you doing to reinforce that image that you see in the mirror each day? Is what you are doing in your workouts consistent with just an image, or is your time spent each workout enhancing and honing skills that will keep you and your partners safe and alive? Are you gearing your PT toward an individual sport, to the point of neglecting other aspects of your fitness that are more germane to what you do on your job each day?

Let me give you an example. I've seen officers that love to pump iron. They would spend five days per week at the gym bench-pressing incredible amounts of weight that resulted in huge upper body size. The problem is that these same guys spend little or no time at all on cardiovascular workouts, nor did they concern themselves with any physical coordination type exercises. Essentially, these guys were bench press machines. They were as strong as an ox. However, when it came time to bail out of the car to chase a bad guy down the street, they are spent after one block. Chase someone up several flights of stairs and then subdue and cuff them...for someone with no cardio in his or her program, that's enough to bend them over in exhaustion. Another example—I am partnered with an officer who is a big runner. He or she runs up to ten miles per day, competes in marathons and other races. When it comes time to bail out with this partner, they have no problem running down the suspect. It's when the bad guy refuses to be cuffed that the runner has the problem. Running everyday, but not doing any upper body or strength training, has caused this officer to be weak and a liability on the street. He or she may run quite efficiently, using very little energy, but when it comes to important tasks like DT's, they are at a disadvantage, lacking sufficient upper body strength.

It is natural for someone to practice and enjoy something that they can do well. That officer that can bench press tons of weight with ease, enjoys doing that and strives to continue to improve on that skill. The officer who is a fantastic runner constantly strives to become even better. But what about something that he or she is not as proficient in? How about having that runner include upper body work several times per week to compliment that excellent cardio workout? Why not include pull-ups, dips, and pushups? For the guy or gal that loves the iron, why not include running or biking to that routine? Yes, I know that the big complaint is that they will lose size by doing that, but cross training not only evens out your body's balance of strength and cardio, but it is directly associated with everything that we do as cops. We chase bad guys, fight with them, subdue and cuff them. Even when we are not involved in direct conflict with someone, we routinely walk, climb, lift, push, and otherwise use ourselves for a myriad of physical things each day.

Now let's bring this training into another area where we need to maintain proficiency--firearms. A firearm, like fitness, is a skill that may potentially save our own or someone else's life. Just as some of us may be better at certain exercises, so also are we sometimes better at different types of shooting and with certain types of weapons. Once again, the human tendency is to practice those things that we do well, more than the ones that we have difficulty with. I know from experience as a firearms instructor that poor bull's-eye shooters will rarely ever practice that discipline unless directed to do so, or if a qualification is imminent. That same shooter may enjoy and perform better at shooting more traditional qualification courses and focus on that strength, rather than the ones in which he or she is deficient. The shotgun, which is traditionally more difficult for instructors to teach and for many students to master, is another area in which officers spend less time. Why? The answer is simply because the shotgun is harder to get comfortable with, and to become proficient in. I rarely had any officer request additional shotgun time after the regular firearms session was over. On the other hand, I constantly had requests for more handgun time.

So that person who you see in the mirror each morning, the one who is buff, sexy, fit, and in your own estimation, tactically superior to most others, is *not* who other people see. What "we" see is someone lacking in certain areas, yet strong in others. We see a good officer who could be an even better officer if only he or she would round out their training to include those things that they don't do as well. None of us are perfect; each one of us has areas in which we need to improve, be it fitness, firearms, DT, tactics, or any other discipline. Get a wakeup call; look at yourself through the prism of reality. Recognize that you need to work harder at certain things that are difficult for you to master. Conversely, less time need be spent on those things that come naturally for you and at which you are already proficient. Never be satisfied with that person looking back at you. Challenge him or her each day to become better, quicker, stronger, smarter, or even more compassionate. If after you read this article and tomorrow you find yourself content with that image that you see, call your optometrist—it's time for an eye exam!

TOO MUCH TECHNOLOGY

Are we putting ourselves at risk by having too many gadgets?

I just finished reading an article in my local newspaper, The Free-Lance Star, which described a new electronic ticketing system now in use by our town's police department. The high tech device allows an officer to scan the barcode on a traffic violator's drivers license. The data is automatically analyzed by the machine, which then inputs the information onto the ticket. Once the form is complete, the officer prints copies of the ticket from a printer, which is located between the two front seats. He then goes forward to have the violator sign the ticket. The advantages over handwritten tickets are obvious. First, the process is quick; the form is complete in seconds. Moreover, there is no chance the ticket will be illegible, a perennial problem with written reports.

However, reading about this latest piece of technology got me thinking. How many more pieces of electronic equipment can we fit inside such a small compartment? Moreover, how much attention will be needed to monitor and operate all of it? I'm not so much concerned about the electronics themselves, except to the extent that they interfere with our ability to be in touch with our surroundings. Recent incidents involving officers ambushed in their vehicles, especially at night, gave me pause to think that perhaps we are setting up a perfect storm for the bad guys to get the jump on us.

What immediately came to mind was the incident in the

state of Washington on Halloween night. Two Seattle cops were in their patrol car reviewing paper work, when a knuckle dragger drove by and opened fire. One officer was killed; his partner was wounded. Just one month later, in the same area, four officers were murdered while they sat in a coffee shop. Granted they weren't killed while in their police vehicles, but they were distracted, nevertheless, by focusing on their laptops, putting them further behind the action v. reaction power curve.

Today's patrol vehicles are loaded with so much gear that it's difficult for an officer to observe and absorb what's going on around him. Take a look in most cars and you will probably find the following equipment: dashboard cam; hand-held or mounted speed enforcement tool; mobile computer terminal; console with radio, lights, and siren controls; department issued and/or personal cell phone; gun rack; electronic traffic ticket device; printer; fingerprint reader; and finally, individual gear bag. That's a ton of stuff to operate and keep track of while trying to drive and/or watch for violations and bad guys.

There is no question that all of the above innovations have enhanced our ability to do our job quickly and efficiently. We've eliminated the middleman to some extent—not having to wait for name checks and license plates to be run by dispatch, etc. Nevertheless, it seems to me that we sometimes pay too much attention to the electronic side of the house, rather than the people side. We pull someone over or detain someone and we can't wait to get back inside the unit to "run" the guy on our terminal. That's great if you've already used your skills to question the guy, get a read on his body language, his eyes, speech pattern, etc. But perhaps younger cops in particular may defer to use the electronics first, rather than stare a hole in the perp and see what reaction he gives. Maybe some of our street smarts are being lost in this tsunami of new technology.

Back in the day, when all we had was the police radio and "good time" radio in cars, we were cautioned by our bosses and old timers not to use the good time radio—it was too much of a distraction. Even though the car radio only had AM stations, nevertheless, guys turned them on. This made for some missed radio assignments, and who knows how much else we didn't hear by not tuning our ears to the street.

What I presently see as a huge threat to officer safety is the laptop computer. Utilizing it takes a significant amount of concentration. Anytime we must focus on anything inside our cars, rather than outside of them, we put ourselves at risk. What really scares me is when I see a unit at night, either on patrol or parked, with the officer inside, lit up by the computer screen. Talk about a target... From a tactical standpoint, sitting stationary at night, filling out a report with the interior illuminating the officer, is a recipe for disaster. I cringe whenever I see it, but that's a whole other issue. My personal opinion is that paperwork is best done at the station, at least in the context of officer safety.

Don't get me wrong—I'm not bashing technology—it's a wonderful thing. Better weaponry, safer body armor, stronger radios, all the improvements that have been made in policing have changed the face of law enforcement. But with change comes some unwelcome results as well. My purpose here is not to bash technology, but to alert us to what new challenges need to be overcome by virtue of their arrival. Not all change is entirely good, some of it has a downside. It's up to each of us to recognize that and prepare to overcome the negatives.

TRAINERS IN NAME ONLY

Five Characteristics of Highly Successful Trainers

All of us in law enforcement and the military have been through some type of training. Our first exposure was at either the police academy or boot camp. This can be a pivotal moment in one's career depending on how the cadre of trainers imparts information to those in their charge. No matter how short or long it has been since you were either in recruit school or in-service training, all of us have vivid images of two types of trainers. The first group we categorize as poor trainers. This group includes trainers that are crude, crass, politically incorrect, lacking in credibility, and ineffective. The second category is those that I characterize as "priceless." These folks are an asset to their department and cause their students to become invigorated about the training, to the extent that their organization will save money, time, or lives as a result. Let's explore five traits that define highly successful trainers.

The High Energy Trainer

This trainer is always on top of his/her game, giving his all in each class without regard to personal matters, administrative matters, weather, space, equipment, etc. These are high-energy type folks. Whenever they face adversity that would normally interfere with teaching, they drive on through, giving their students the information they will need to successfully complete and master the course. Given a choice of training classes to attend, this trainer's class always fills up first. There is never an empty chair in his/her classroom.

The Recognized Expert

Constant research, self-improvement, testing, publishing articles, and networking make this trainer an expert in his/her field. Unlike the officer that goes to an instructor class and never updates his information or attends re-certification classes, the recognized expert keeps abreast of the latest technical information through classes and manuals. By either observing while in the field, or talking with those who are, this instructor is constantly re-evaluating tactics, techniques, and methods that will either work successfully, or cause officers to be put at risk. The recognized expert is also utilized in court to prove or disprove a point for the prosecuting attorney. He/she is highly respected in the LE community.

The Teaches That Doesn't Regurgitate

I think that we have all seen this type of instructor. This person simply parrots or reads a script or PowerPoint presentation provided to them by someone else. After the first five minutes of this instructor's class, most students are either on their way to dreamland or finishing a report that was due yesterday. This person lacks drive and initiative. He is not spontaneous, shies away from questions, and generally can't wait until the class is over. Conversely, the instructor that actually teaches is animated, energetic, spontaneous, and invites student participation. He will sometimes fail to cover all of the material in the allotted time due to attendees' participation and input regarding the subject matter. Students hang on this instructor's every word and often stay after class has ended to further discuss points that were raised during the session.

The Inspirational Instructor

I take the liberty of borrowing a motto from the Marine Corps: "Earned Never Given," referring to the fact that the title of Marine must be earned; it will not be given to just anyone. The same holds true for the instructor who insists that his/her students learn the subject matter before given a certificate of completion or title of instructor. Many courses only require that the person have attended the session; certificates earned through these courses are meaningless. A good example of this is the officer sent to an instructor course, returns to the department, and then never teaches one class on the topic. Instructors who are "worth their weight in gold" ensure that before anyone graduates or completes their course, the student must demonstrate that they have mastered the material or techniques. The best trainers inspire their students to "want" to learn. When a student completes or graduates from a class given by the highly successful trainer, they prize that certificate or instructor label for they recognize that it was not simply handed to them—they earned it.

The High Return Rate Instructor

There are instructors out there that sometimes have the same students returning to attend their classes. It may be either a different class that they are teaching, or even one that they have previously attended. Why would someone do that? Simply because the highly effective instructor engenders a feeling of excitement and energy that is infectious to all that know him/her. Once you have been through one of these individual's classes, you can't wait to return for another. These instructors build their students up, infusing them with the desire to improve constantly on their classroom technique, delivery, testing, and evaluation. They are role models that have created instructor paradigms for those that love to teach. They are a fountain of information; they are a resource that never runs dry.

Do you possess any or all of the aforementioned characteristics? Are you presently a trainer, or are you contemplating becoming one? If the answer is yes, be aware that to become a highly effective trainer involves hard work. In many cases, it involves taking on extra assignments in addition to your regularly assigned duties. It means preparing lesson plans on your own time, buying supplies or equipment with your own money because your agency refuses to purchase them, sometimes even working a double shift or on your scheduled day off. A good trainer willingly makes these sacrifices, accepting them as part of the job. Would life be simpler for the trainer without these obstacles? The answer is yes, but then the job would be easy and anyone could do it. The trick is to do the job well in spite of them, without becoming disillusioned or jaded. Can you do it? If you can, then join the ranks of highly effective trainers—if you think you are strong enough. The rewards are, for the most part, intangible, but that means they are not man-made--they are matters of the heart.

WARRIORS IN HIGH HEELS

Don't test their mettle

A crazed gunman walks into a building in Fort Hood, Texas, pulls out two handguns, and begins firing indiscriminately at everyone and everything. Two cops respond, one of whom is a female, and they both engage the subject as he leaves. Despite being shot in both legs, she continued to fight on.

In Seattle, a pair of cops are seated in their patrol car reviewing reports. Suddenly, a car pulls next to their unit and begins firing at them, killing the male officer and wounding the female partner. She returns fire and summons help, even though she suffered a gunshot wound.

A former police officer from Minneapolis, working security at a church in Colorado, confronts a gunman who has already shot several people. She finds cover and waits for her opportunity to take him down. She identifies herself and engages the man, fatally shooting him.

These are but a few of the recent incidents in which our sisters in uniform have distinguished themselves. I shouldn't be amazed at their valor and professionalism, but being old school, I admit that I still harbor an old fashioned image of women and their role in society. It's wrong, I know. I've seen enough ladies in my time who could succeed at just about anything they put their mind to. For example, I had a student in one of my classes at the FBI Academy who suffered a torn ACL, which is one of the four major ligaments in the knee. This injury occurred two weeks before graduation, and just days before the final firearms qualification. She was told that if she failed to qualify with her weapon, she would not graduate.

Amazingly, this young woman had a remarkable ability to focus on her goal. She wound up wrapping her knee and putting on a brace. On the day of the final qualification course, which included running from one yard marker to another, shooting from the prone, kneeling, and standing positions, she somehow managed to complete the course and qualify. Believe me when I tell you that I wasn't the only one whose jaw dropped at the final whistle. It was one of the more gutsy performances I've ever witnessed. She went on to graduate and receive her credentials as an FBI Agent.

I spent some time as a DT/PT Instructor at the academy. At one point, one of my female colleagues was pregnant, and as time went by and the baby grew, I thought that she would relinquish her duties on the mat and take on a more admin type role. Boy was I wrong. This woman continued with her normal teaching schedule, which included leading her class in PT and teaching defensive tactics. The curriculum included arrest techniques and ground fighting skills. I was reluctant to co-teach with her, thinking that I might injure her or the baby. She quickly disabused my of that notion, and rolled around on the ground with me as we demo'd mount and guard positions, escapes, and weapon retention. What an inspiration. I've known guys who've pulled themselves from class when they had a headache. Talk about wimping out...

It's all illustrative of a couple of points that I continue to make throughout the course of many of the articles I write for this website and others. There are several reasons why these women performed as they did. The main one is they reverted to their training. That old, irrefutable axiom—the way you train is the way you fight—is clearly at work here. When things go sideways, when you find yourself in the midst of a critical situation, your only recourse is to summon what you've learned in training. It becomes your frame of reference. If you've trained for all of the possibilities, the "what ifs," then you've more than likely embedded a memory of the incident and how to handle it somewhere in that big storage cabinet we call our brain.

This was never more evident than when Seattle Officer Britt Sweeny found herself involved in a shooting incident that killed her partner. Seattle Assistant Chief of Police described her actions as "those of a ten year veteran." Inasmuch as she was fresh from the academy, her recent training was all she had to rely on. She not only returned fire after being wounded, but she got on the air and put out a description of the offender. That's pretty darn good for a rookie.

But there's more to all of this than just training. There's something much deeper, something intangible that many of these female warriors exhibit. It's their spirit; it's their inner strength. It's self confidence in knowing that they possess the tools, knowledge, and the ability to do the job, regardless of any obstacles they may encounter. This warrior attitude imbues them with fortitude and strength, similar to that of a mother bear who protects her cubs from harm. They don't know the words, "can't, won't, or fail." They attack with a frightful ferocity that I'm certain the bad guys never imagined might emanate from such a tiny adversary.

Are there female cops who I absolutely would not work with? You bet, but I've also had my share of male officers who I wouldn't go through a door with either. Our sisters in blue have proven that they belong. Anyone who questions their skills and abilities doesn't have a clue. When they put that uniform on, get into that vest, and hitch up their duty belt, they rightly take their place on the front lines.

Sadly, there's also a downside to the emergence of these female paladins. As they increasingly interject themselves in more violent confrontations, they sometimes lose the battle. The latest figures show that 223 female police officers have been killed in the line of duty, their names inscribed on the wall at the National Law Enforcement Memorial in Washington, DC. And as I write this article, I'm aware that another name will soon be added to that list, that of Officer Tina Griswold, Lakewood, Washington PD. She and three of her colleagues were ambushed and murdered at a coffee shop. The devil does indeed walk among us.

If you're one of those who still question whether female cops belong on the job, I'm here to tell you that they most certainly do. They can perform the job as well as, or better than many of us. But here's the bottom line: it's not a question of gender with regard to who can do the job of policing. Rather, it's a question of heart. Who can devote their life to being a **career** warrior. That's right, not dedicate their life to a **job**. Being a cop is a vocation, a calling, if you will. You don't take the job simply because it pays well, or has great benefits. You become a cop because you believe in, and stand for, good over evil, right over wrong, principle over expediency. If you're on the job for any other reason, you're not in it to win it.

WARRIORS IN HIGH HEELS, PART II

How do their deaths affect society?

I pen this article on Memorial Day, 2010, a sacrosanct occasion that I hope politicians never try to change or abolish, like they've done with other important days in our nation's history. This morning while I was working out, I tuned in to a local radio talk show. The host and his listeners were discussing the recent phenomenon of female soldiers killed in combat. He posed this question to his audience: Does the fact that we send women into combat enhance society, or degrade it? My gut instinct was that it improved our society and culture, but I listened to some callers who were convinced that women have no place on the battlefield.

An article in the _Sunday Washington Post_, dated 5/30/2010, revealed some interesting statistics that may surprise some of you. During World War II, American servicewomen suffered sixteen combat deaths; Vietnam produced only one. However, deaths from the wars in the Middle East have resulted in eighty U.S. servicewomen killed due to hostile action, more than from any other causes, such as accidents. The numbers have risen because women are directly involved in fighting, even though officially they are barred. Operating as fighter pilots, EOD techs, helicopter gunship pilots, platoon leaders, and machine-gunners on convoys, women are in the thick of the fight. You can't be in these types of positions and not be in harm's way.

As I continued to listen to callers to the radio show, people on both sides of the argument opined, some strident in their assertion that women belonged at home. Didn't children need their mothers? I instantly yelled at the radio: *Kids need their fathers just as much!* Others took the position that the feminist movement was the cause of this morphing of a woman's role in society. That's a hot-button issue that I wouldn't touch, but as I thought further about the issue, I found myself taking the position that women in military combat were no different than our female police officers on the streets of our cities and towns.

In January of this year, I wrote an article entitled, <u>Warriors In High Heels</u>. In it, I described some of the more recent events in which women played a pivotal role in saving lives. Some of the incidents resulted in the officer losing her life, something which all of us know can occur once we pin on the badge. Female police officers, just like their male colleagues, serve on the front lines, 24/7. They sometimes find themselves in situations which are life threatening. Do we ban them from police work because the possibility exists that they might be killed? Of course not. We expect they will react accordingly, based on the training we've given them—the same training we've given their male colleagues.

Then the talk show host posed this question: Is it worse when a female servicewoman is killed in the line of duty; is it a degradation of society when we send women to fight for our country? After all, we've become accustomed to men losing their lives on the battlefield, but women . . . ?

Let me make a point here. In Israel, every physically able citizen, men *and* women, must serve in the army for three years. In contrast, the U.S. is fortunate to have an all-volunteer fighting force. Men and women who join the armed forces in our country are serving because they want to, not because the government has compelled them. Women who join do so of their own volition—even those in combat. I see no difference in women who join either a police department or the military, both recognize they will be physically challenged, and are up to the task. Indeed, some of our female warriors are doing both simultaneously—serving in the military and the police force. None of these women is looking for sympathy or shortcuts. They know that respect is earned, never given. They don't countenance playing favorites, they expect to do the job. When one of our women in uniform loses her life, whether their garb is military or police, we mourn the loss for what it is—a fallen warrior.

Does it make a difference if the death is that of a male or female? Of course not; both are equally mourned, no one sex takes precedence over the other. The loss of a husband, wife, mother, or father, is devastating. Ask any family who has suffered such a tragedy, and they will simply tell you they've lost a family member. It matters not whether that loved one was a man or a woman.

In the United States there are 900,000 law enforcement officers protecting you and me every day. Twelve per cent of that complement is female. They serve proudly, and fearlessly face danger from knuckle-draggers who would just as soon kill them as any male officer. In fact, according to the National Law Enforcement Memorial, 237 female officers have been killed in the line of duty. They've made the ultimate sacrifice; they've paid the price.

Women in combat—good or bad? My answer: a resounding good. I've trained women in PT/DT, and in firearms, and I've seen them react under stress. I've gone through doors with them and worked alongside them on protracted surveillances. Some have whined, as have some men, most have simply steeled themselves to the challenge. To withhold them from serving on the battlefield is a mistake and dishonors the memory of those who have fallen. To over-react when one of them is killed is to pay a disservice to those willing and able to serve. If you've ever seen a mother bear defending her cubs, you have an idea of how ferocious our warriors in high heels can become. We need them on the front lines.

Links:
Washington Post:
http://www.washingtonpost.com/wp-dyn/content/article/2010/05/29/AR2010052903618.html

Officer.com article:
http://www.officer.com/web/online/Police-Life/Warriors-in-High-Heels/17$50011

National Law Enforcement Memorial:
http://www.nleomf.org/facts/enforcement/

WHY MORE OF US ARE BEING KILLED

What you can do to reverse the trend

As I write this article the number of police officers killed in the line of duty in 2007 has increased almost 30%; 170 cops gone—end of watch. This coincides with a rise in violent crime, according to the FBI, after a period of 15 years in which we experienced a decline. Why the increase? What changes have occurred in our job in the way of training, deployment, equipment, and weapons that have caused these deaths to increase? I think that there are several reasons why we are dying in higher numbers, but they are factors that we can change if we have the courage and fortitude to do so.

Police as a first line of defense

Our police departments serve as the first line of defense against those that would disregard our laws and do harm to any of our citizens. There are, and there will always be, cretins among us that want what we have but are not willing to acquire those things in a lawful manner. These knuckle draggers feel no remorse for their crimes; they have no conscience. These types need to be permanently removed from society. The court system has coddled these criminals for as long as I can remember, refusing to make them accountable for their actions. Instead, they have assigned counselors, and other social service types, to explain away the reasons why these Neanderthals have raped, robbed, and murdered our families, friends, and neighbors. Some of the imbecilic reasons these do-gooders come up with are so absurd that you almost have to laugh at them or you would fall over in disbelief.

The community has handcuffed the police, rather than the bad guys, so that we fear repercussions from our leaders and legislators more than we fear going head to head with the Satan-like law breakers. Policies that force the street cop to have to ask permission to use a Taser are a product of social engineers wanting "everyone to just get along." Not having shields available in each car is indefensible. Why do we keep equipment locked up in trunks of supervisors' cars or in equipment rooms at the station, instead of deploying them on the street? Why are we adopting policies that cause our first responders to hold back, rather than go in and take care of business? I can remember when the street cop responded to any call and handled it. He may have requested additional help or detectives, but he did it in the middle of the battle, not from a block or two away. At a time when criminals feel emboldened by a lack of punishment, and fear neither the courts nor us, our response is becoming increasingly encumbered by layers of bureaucracy and time-consuming policies.

Excess baggage

Our training is better than it has ever been. Our weapons, both lethal and less-lethal, are almost always appropriate for the situation at hand. Our men and women continue to be

America's finest—not backing down from any fight. But never before have they had to carry so much baggage! As I go around the country teaching use of force, there is a common theme that is evident when an officer explains why he either did not use deadly force, or he delayed using it—he thought about the legal repercussions. What would the newspaper do with the story; what would the community do to him if he shot someone? I even see this hesitation when using less-lethal weapons, such as Taser and OC spray. And, as much as I explain how important it is to gain the upper hand, as much as I talk about action versus reaction, the prevailing attitude is that they will wait. It is mind-boggling that these otherwise fine officers will put themselves at risk for fear of what the people that they are ultimately protecting will think of them.

Supervisors not cops

I am not sure at which level of supervisory rank this anomaly occurs, but my sense is that it begins at the position of lieutenant. This does not apply to all, as I personally know a watch commander in Nevada that spends more time on the street being a cop than spending time in the station. But generally at that stage the management mindset begins to take precedence over being a cop. Things like manpower, timesheets, report writing, disciplinary hearings, etc., cause the supervisor to put being a cop on the back burner. This mindset becomes more evident as we go up the chain, and at each level the job of being a cop becomes inexorably conjoined with social work. Instead of backing a cop for subduing or shooting a thug, they abdicate their responsibility to their fellow cops, and try to assuage the phony and trumped up outrage that some innocuous, self-proclaimed community representative spouts to any media type that will listen.

There are exceptions. Several years ago in the metro Washington, D.C. area, Police Chief Charles Ramsey and Assistant Chief Terry Gainer, would prowl the streets of D.C. at night, putting thugs on the wall and responding to in-progress radio assignments. Talk about backing your fellow cops...

Warrior Cops

This may not sound politically correct, but we have to create and spread the mindset that our street cops are modern day warriors. As such, they will sometimes need to be tough, demanding, over-bearing, and over-powering. They need to immediately dominate a situation and gain control. They have to be allowed to err on the side of a little too much force, rather than too little. The bad guys are used to a more laid back cop mindset now. They know that the cop fears the press and community more than they fear him. The creeps know that society will let them commit the same crimes over and over again, without having to pay much of a price (or none at all) for their behavior. In the process, if they hurt or kill a cop, it changes nothing. Cop killers are rarely put to death. Indeed, some become celebrities—writing books, and having movies made about them that glamorize their wicked ways. And what of the cop that was maimed or killed? After two or three days of obligatory coverage, the cops and their families fade into the background to fend for themselves, never to be heard from again.

Change starts with you

So how do we turn this thing around? We do it one cop at a time. We do it by being unafraid to say something that society has deemed "politically incorrect," but we know to be absolutely right. We speak up about ridiculous PC classes that we are forced to attend on how to talk to certain segments of society so as not to hurt their feelings. We do it by not being afraid to ask tough questions of people on the street, or for that matter, of our administration and community. The old axiom that states "There are no atheists in foxholes," is analogous to one that states, "There are no victims that are pro-criminal." Until someone has become a victim of a crime, or a member of their family has suffered at the hands of a street thug, they will continue to wrongly assume that the criminal has more rights than the average citizen. If you don't believe me, explain to me why it is necessary that we have programs such as "Victim's Rights" and "Victim Assistance." The reason is that we pay too much attention to ensuring that the criminal has every right and comfort afforded to him, while we harass, brow-beat, inconvenience, intimidate, and otherwise embarrass the victims. It is unconscionable what we put these poor folks through, while ensuring that the poor criminal that has hurt, humiliated, and stolen from them, has enough to eat, is warm, and has a proper defense to answer the charges brought against him.

We should all be outraged at this juxtaposition, but we have been conditioned to accept it as "the right thing to do." I propose we begin to fight back in whatever way that we can. We have been led like sheep to the slaughter, afraid to say anything unpopular. In the process, we have given away much of the power that we had as cops. We simply drive around, afraid to assert ourselves, indeed, sometimes even afraid to defend ourselves for fear of what the morning's headlines might say.

Why are more of us being killed? Because we allow it!

WILL YOU BE READY?

Your test comes like a thief in the night.

Have you ever known anyone who went to their doctor and was, unfortunately, given the terrible news that they had a terminal illness? When they were told they had six months or a year to live, did they just give up and go home to die? Probably not. If you have known one of these individuals, you know they drastically changed their lives for their remaining days on earth. They completely changed priorities, putting themselves and their families first. Things that they thought were important before—jobs, projects, material things—moved way down on the list of what used to consume most of their time. Now what gained prominence were things like: places they had always wanted to visit, things they had always wanted to try, people they had always wanted to meet, and even things they had always wanted to say. They also, perhaps for the very first time, faced their mortality and very likely began a dialogue with the Lord unlike any they have ever had before.

Now, let's move this same scenario from the medical field to the law enforcement domain. Imagine if you will, that you knew the exact date and time that you would be involved in a fight for your life—a gun battle. Let us presume that in exactly six months from now, at exactly 3:00 pm, you knew that you would engage a bad guy in a gunfight. Tell me what you would be doing from the moment that you learned this challenge would take place, until the actual event occurred. Never mind...I know your answer—you would be training day and night to prepare yourself for this life and death struggle. You would recognize that on your daily list of priorities, training to win has just superseded all else that you used to think was important. You would ensure that your marksmanship, tactics, equipment, strength and health, were all "spot on." When that date and time finally arrived, chances are you would be the most efficient fighting machine that you could possibly imagine.

We know that the aforementioned scenario could never take place. That being said, if you will never know exactly when such a critical incident might occur, but know that your job as a police officer carries a high probability that you may be involved in a gun battle on any given day, why aren't you preparing yourself for that moment? Why do many of us, including our administrators, place a low priority on training? Why is it that whenever there is a budget crunch, the first area to take a hit is the training dollar? The paradox is that everyone recognizes the value of training, we all concur that training saves lives, yet we are quick to eliminate it from the budget at the first hint of a monetary crunch. So that begs the question...Will you be ready when your test presents itself, and how do you prepare? There are three areas of preparation: **physical, mental,** and **spiritual.**

PHYSICAL

Physical preparation involves first, your individual fitness. This is an area, which no one else bears responsibility but you. You need to be doing something in this area each day. The very nature of our job demands that you be fit. We chase after people, we confront non-compliant subjects, we lift and carry people, we are more often than not performing physical tasks each shift. If we are unfit, these things become a liability for us and our colleagues. If I am chasing a subject up several flights of stairs, when I catch him I still have to have the strength to cuff him. I also expect that my partner(s) will be right there with me as well. Fitness does not mean that you have to be a competitive bodybuilder or marathoner, but it requires that you occasionally challenge yourself and get your heart rate elevated. If you never stress your body, when you encounter a stressful incident on the street there is a high probability that you will fail.

Physical also includes being instinctively familiar with your weapons and weapon systems. It means through training, being able to get to and manipulate every tool on your duty belt without thinking or looking at any of it. Being physically prepared also means being effective with that service weapon, shoulder weapon, and less-lethal weapon when the need presents itself.

MENTAL

Mental preparation means being focused on duty. It means not bringing any baggage with you from home or anywhere else. That argument that you had with your spouse or child last night needs to be shelved while you focus on the task. Mental preparation includes having a "can-do" mentality that translates into a mind-set that gives you the confidence that you can handle anything at any time. Not over confidence, but rather the piece of mind that comes with knowing you have covered all the bases.

One other aspect of mental preparation involves that gray matter that we sometimes neglect. It is incumbent on each of us to stay current with the means and methods that will allow us to perform our jobs as efficiently and expertly as possible. That means constantly talking with our colleagues and doing our own research about new products, training techniques, and tactics that have been performed successfully by other police officers. It also means not waiting for the training officer to deliver all of our training. Sometimes we need to be proactive and actually train ourselves when it is obvious that our department cannot provide us with all the tools that will likely keep us alive. Finally, it involves going over in our mind the "what ifs" that may possibly cross our path this day or any day, and the plan that we have to win those situations.

SPIRITUAL

The last level of preparation is the spiritual component. It is no coincidence that most departments have police chaplains. These dedicated men and women minister to our every need, but most importantly, they are there in times of line of duty deaths and serious injuries. Spirituality has always played a role in law enforcement. Each year recall that there is a national ceremony in Washington, D.C., that commemorates our fallen comrades, which includes a mass said in their honor. Ensure that your spiritual house is in order so that when you walk out of roll call you leave nothing to chance. When body, mind, and spirit are in tune, you are a righteous warrior, not unlike Michael the Archangel, patron saint of police officers.

Will you be ready? I pray that you are, because, just like the thief that comes in the night, you never know when your test will come.

Stay safe, brothers and sisters!

OTHER TITLES BY JOHN M. WILLS

- Title: Midnight Battles in the windy city
- Series: A Chicago Warriors™ Thriller
- Author: John M. Wills
- Price: $27.95
- Publisher: TotalRecall Publications, Inc.
- Format: HARDCOVER, 6.14" x 9.21"
- Number of pages: 352
- 13-digit ISBN: 978-1-59095-843-8
- Publication: 2009

Chicago Police Officer Pete Shannon's life is about to take a dramatic turn. His wife has a dark secret that she's about to reveal to him; his partner's life is about to be in jeopardy, and worst of all one of his own colleagues will present him with one of the biggest challenges of his life. Pete's strength, both physical and spiritual, will be put to the test as he and his partner work the "graveyard shift" on the mean streets of the "Windy City."

Fellow officer Marilyn Benson doesn't realize it yet, but her life is about to change in ways that she could have never imagined. Forces of good and evil will do battle for her soul and her faith, both of which have lain dormant for many years. It's an issue that she can no longer ignore. St. Michael the Archangel, patron saint of police officers, is about to engage in his biggest clash since throwing Satan out of Heaven.

Praise

"I spent a lot of years with John Wills in the law enforcement trenches of Detroit, a place where Christian faith is rarely a survivor. Somehow John's flourished. In Chicago Warriors, he has created a unique narrative demonstrating how the worst of man can be defeated by the best in man."

*--**Paul Lindsay**, author of The Fuhrer's Reserve, Traps, The Big Scam, Freedom to Kill, and Witness to the Truth.*

"Wills covers issues that are timely today, including date rape, violence associated with prostitutes, steroid use among body builders, young criminals and police corruption.... There is no problem with language, sexual content or violence."

*-- **Marilyn Olsen**, President of Public Safety Writers Association*

"Chicago Warriors is the true voice of a battle tested street cop. A real cop's words, a real cop's experiences, John Wills knows how to tell a story!"

*-- **Randy Sutton**, Author of "A COP'S LIFE", and "TRUE BLUE*

"*Midnight Battles in the Windy City* explores the dark underside of police work while illustrating the characters' moral values--all under the greater theme of good versus evil."

*-- **Andrea Nealon**, Free Lance Star Reporter*

"What a great story! *Chicago Warriors* is a wonderful, inspirational read, and it was hard to keep a dry eye throughout. John Wills puts in words what every law enforcement officer knows in his heart...that forces of evil roam the earth and oftentimes ordinary men and women behind a badge have first contact. As a retired federal agent and author, like John, I have called upon Saint Michael to pull me through many perils like the characters in his book."

*-- **Mike Angley**, Author of the Child Finder Series*

"The story carried me along. The characters are like so many I've met over the years. You know you're reading a good police novel when you go to work and find that: life imitates the art you're reading.

*-- **Dean C. Kavouras**, Police Chaplain*

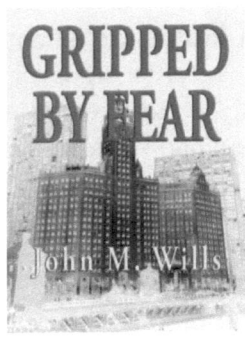

- Title: Gripped By Fear
- Series: A Chicago Warriors™ Thriller
- Author: John M. Wills
- Price: $27.95
- Publisher: TotalRecall Publications, Inc.
- Format: HARDCOVER, 6.14" x 9.21"
- Number of pages: 288
- 13-digit ISBN: 978-1-59095-772-1
- Publication: 2010

Pete Shannon and Marilyn Benson find themselves working their biggest case yet in their new role as Chicago Police Detectives. In this second book of the Chicago Warrior Thriller Series, a madman has inexplicably targeted women who labor as office cleaners in downtown Chicago, sexually assaulting them as they travel to and from their job.

As the number of victims begins to mount, the two investigators are pressured by their boss to solve this horrendous crime pattern. Local community organizations soon stage protest rallies at City Hall, convincing the media that the city has become "gripped by fear" as a result of the rapes. The Mayor demands quick action by the Police Superintendent to end this reign of terror. The heat is on, as summer in Chicago begins to sizzle, forcing the two detectives to put their lives on the line as they attempt to capture this demon of the darkness.

In the midst of it all, Marilyn learns some disturbing news that forces her to choose between her loyalty to Pete and the man she loves....and in the dramatic climax Marilyn's Christian faith plays a major role in saving her life.

Praise

Once again John Wills delivers a nitty-gritty true-to-life "you can taste the atmosphere" story about the life of police officers on the often violent streets of Chicago. Captured in the language and with a feel that only a cop from Chicago can deliver, *Gripped By Fear*, second of the Chicago Warrior Thrillers, reveals some of the heroism, fears, motivation and courage cops everywhere can relate to.

Frank Borelli, *Editor in Chief of Officer.com*

"*Gripped by Fear* is as authentic as it gets. John Wills brings all of his law enforcement experience as well as his writing skills together to bring us a terrific read."

*--***Lt. Randy Sutton,** *Las Vegas Metro PD's "most highly decorated officer in department history"; Author of True Blue and A Cops Life Law Enforcement Commentator, Fox News*

"*Gripped by Fear* is Christian fiction's equivalent of Law and Order: gritty yet filled with hope in the ultimate triumph, delivering a thrilling read that Christian readers will appreciate."

*--***Alex Jurek,** *INDenverTimes.com*

"...*Gripped by Fear* is a not only a good mystery but also an exploration of the many challenges faced by today's law enforcement officers. It will be of special interest to readers who enjoy books with a strong Christian theme."

*--***Marilyn Olsen,** *President, Public Safety Writers Association*

"John Wills...takes you to the heart and soul of the Chicago undercover police force...taking note of every movement, every sound, things out of place—details only a veteran of law enforcement could provide. Woven through this police thriller is an inspirational message of faith. *Gripped by Fear* is a great read and a book you won't want to miss."

*--***Margaret Oleska,** *Richmond Book Examiner*

- Title: Targeted
- Series: A Chicago Warriors™ Thriller
- Author: John M. Wills
- Price: $27.95
- Publisher: TotalRecall Publications, Inc.
- Format: HARDCOVER, 6.14" x 9.21"
- Number of pages: 346
- 13-digit ISBN: 978-1-59095-794-3
- Publication: 2011

Chicago Police Detectives Pete Shannon and Marilyn Benson are thrust into a homicide investigation, taking them away from the Violent Crimes Unit where they are normally assigned. A crazed gunman has been targeting cops, killing them for no apparent reason, other than for his own deranged satisfaction. The duo find themselves teamed with a pair of tough talking, abrasive, seasoned cops who do their best to interfere with the young detectives at every juncture, making their lives miserable. The hunt for the serial killer becomes a life-altering experience for the partners as they face individual challenges that threaten to destroy them.

At the same time, **Father Ed Matthews, a Catholic priest,** has been accused of child molestation at the southwest side parish where he's assigned. Pete and Marilyn arrest him, but as the priest begins his journey through the Chicago judicial system, he decides to flee the city and become a fugitive. He begins a journey away from the priesthood from which he may never return.

Praise

"*Targeted* will grab you and not let go. A must read for all mystery / suspense / thriller enthusiasts"
-- **Paul Lindsay,** *author of five bestselling FBI novels*

"Wills writes about the streets of Chicago like only a former Chicago cop could."
-- **Noah Boyd,** *New York Times bestselling author of The Bricklayer*

Targeted is a fascinating behind-the-scenes look at Chicago detectives who are guided by God's hand and mores while struggling to apprehend a serial assassin who's targeting cops. John Wills has crafted a Christian thriller with heart."
-- **Alan Jacobson,** *New York Times bestselling author of Velocity*

"Wills creates a psychopathic serial killer, a terrifying monster, and unleashes him onto the streets of Chicago."
-- **Mark Safarik,** *FBI Criminal Profiler (Ret.) and Director of Forensic Behavioral Services.*

"Wills wrote a thriller with an ending I could not have imagined."
-- **Frank Borelli,** *Editor-in-Chief, Officer.com*

"Retired FBI agent John M. Wills keeps cranking out the books. He's just penned this third suspense novel *Targeted* as part of his "Chicago Warriors Thriller" series. The ex-FBI agent and former Chicago cop has written a novel about a sniper who targets and kills cops in Chicago, rocking the Windy City. As a part of the complex tale, a Catholic priest is arrested for child molestation, but flees Chicago after being freed on bond. The two story lines collide in an unforgettable ending."
-- Review from **Allan Lengel** ticklethewire.com

If you are a Mystery / Detective reader than John M. Wills Chicago Warriors Thriller Series are some of the best titles that I have published for you.
-- **Bruce Moran**, *Publisher*

Contact John: jmwills@hotmail.com
Website: JohnMWills.com

www.ingramcontent.com/pod-product-compliance
Lightning Source LLC
Chambersburg PA
CBHW030327080526
44584CB00012B/752